Goodbye, SPIDER

Marcella Detreville

ISBN 979-8-89112-328-1 (Paperback)
ISBN 979-8-89112-330-4 (Hardcover)
ISBN 979-8-89112-329-8 (Digital)

Unless otherwise stated, all scripture passages came from the New International Version of the Holy Bible.

Covenant Books
11661 Hwy 707
Murrells Inlet, SC 29576
www.covenantbooks.com

CONTENTS

INTRODUCTION

My FOUR-YEAR-OLD GRANDSON had a recurring nightmare for weeks. His parents asked me to talk to him and pray for him because they were sure that the dream was significant. He tearfully told me his dream. He said, "A giant spider came down from the sky, and we all looked at it. It spun a web around our whole family and then stuck us in his web. The giant spider wanted to suck all our lives out one at a time. We cut ourselves out of the web and then chased him away and never let the spider come near our house again."

What a *nightmare*!

Millions of people find themselves stuck in toxic relationships. Even more than toxic are narcissistic-personality-syndrome (NPS) relationships, which are twisted toxic relationships. The mysterious harm is initially difficult to identify, and then a pattern emerges. This book is the result of my own experience with this dynamic, but it is not written as a memoir. It is written as a help for anyone wondering how to identify, escape from, and stay out of the web of the spider (the NPS). This text is largely referring to narcissistic dynamics in intimate relationships. It is also helpful for any toxic relationship.

I wrote this book especially with the Christian community in mind. It is difficult to understand Christian ethics when experiencing insidious abuse and how to respond with biblical wisdom.

I hope to help people identify unhealthy, narcissistic/toxic relationships and also provide a guide for one to extract themselves from harmful behaviors associated with these. Recovery, healing, and a better future are possible when we understand the path to them.

God bless you.

CHAPTER 1

Toxic Relationships— Validation

Toxic relationships seem to be an epidemic these days. Intimate toxic relationships are the most damaging, especially those involving people with *narcissistic personality syndrome* (NPS).

The spider is a simile for the NPS because of its characteristics of spinning a web to catch a target and consuming them at will. Those stuck to and wrapped in this web have hope.

With God's help, our own effort, and some support, we can love freely within safe, healthy relationships. Getting unstuck is the goal, and staying unstuck is a life choice.

Hopefully, this book will assist those trapped in the web of NPS relationships. This book is helpful for recovery from any form of a toxic relationship. Although it is geared strongly toward those involving narcissistic personality syndrome (NPS) and will refer to the person offending or harming as the NPS, it is a good resource to help mitigate and prevent repeat entrapment in toxic relationships.

I will describe narcissistic personality syndrome (NPS) later. Right now I want to help those who need validation that they are in trouble.

Oxford Languages defines *validation* as the action of checking or proving the validity or accuracy of something (OxfordLanguages. org 2022).

The confusion and insidious nature of NPS relationships leaves sufferers feeling crazy, for lack of a better term! Please forgive me for using the term *crazy*, but most who experience this strange relationship say that they feel like they are going crazy! You are not crazy! What you are experiencing is covert abuse. Your abuser is offensive to themselves and you in an ambiguous way.

Nothing is accurate in an NPS relationship because you are bonding with a facade, not a genuine person. When you first bond with your NPS, it is a whirlwind of a wonderful, really gratifying experience, and then something subtly changes. You feel it but cannot prove it. It feels deep and provocative, but evidence is nonexistent. The only evidence that you have is your gut feeling. If you look closely, you'll see very subtle clues that confirm you are in a different state than the loving one that you believed was happening initially. *This is how it all begins.*

Remember DC Comics' Bizarro World? If you have never read comic books, check it out. In the normal universe, all the superheroes were virtuous and wore bright costumes symbolizing justice.

In Bizarro World, the heroes look exactly the same but are cynical and shady. Some clues were darker versions of their original bright uniforms and shady behavior, and instead of doing good, they were wicked.

This is the nature of toxic relationships involving NPS characters. Some people compare their experience to a bad dream. They just want to wake up from the nightmare and get on with the too-good-to-be-true love connection.

Your gut will keep warning you that you are being mistreated. And so you may talk about your feelings to your NPS partner. Initially, they talk you out of your feelings. "I can't believe you think I will do anything to harm or disrespect you. I love you!" They may explode with shock that you think such things. They may sulk or feed you a list of accolades. And for a while, you are soothed, but you can't shake that red flag. You know something is really off!

The decomposition of the relationship continues, and they continue to deny it. In extremely tiny increments, the termites of covert abuse begin to gnaw away at you and your "perfect relationship." The perpetrator convinces you and especially others that nothing is wrong. It is very important that they convince others that all is well. The others are those closest to you. They are the audience—those who observe the facade but also believe that this person is wonderful.

If you go for counseling, the religious counselor may say the devil is accusing this wonderful person. The secular counselor may pull out cookie-cutter methods of open communication with the NPS partner, and then things get worse! This is because the last person you need to spill your guts to is a narcissist. They collect information to use against you later in the relationship.

You are not imagining harm! You are in a difficult, insidious danger. This cannot be handled like normal relationship conflicts because it is extremely abnormal. The narcissistic person has a dysfunctional hard drive that only works for them, not you. You, the clergy, the counselor, or the psychiatrist are not working with normal human reasoning.

Back in the days of radio, there was AM radio first. Later, FM radio was developed. The device, a radio, had an antenna to pick up those AM or FM frequencies. Older radios did not have the interior components to receive FM frequency, so no matter how much tuning a person did, they could not pick up FM stations on AM radios.

Traditional relationship counseling does not work in these relationships because the ability to tune in is absent.

In the movie *Lord of the Rings: The Fellowship of the Ring*, there is a scene in which our heroes heard a strange noise that scared off the creatures they were battling. Gandalf the Gray knew what it was. "It's a Balrog, a demon of the deep," he said. "Swords are of no use here. RUN!"

Before we begin the journey to recovery from NPS abuse, we must accept without validation from the offender that our position is true. It is valid, and it is harmful. From this point, we have the power to change our course to making healthy decisions and healing as we move forward.

> But mark this: There will be terrible times in the last days. People will be lovers of themselves, lovers of money, boastful, proud, abusive, disobedient to their parents, ungrateful, unholy, without love, unforgiving, slanderous, without self-control, brutal, not lovers of the good, treacherous, rash, conceited, lovers of pleasure rather than lovers of God, having a form of godliness but denying its power. *Have nothing to do with such people.* But they will not get very far because, as in the case of those men their folly will be clear to all. (2 Timothy 3:1–5, 3:9; emphasis added)

This passage of Scripture from the Bible describes the character of toxic people in the world now! Anyone can find themselves in this kind of relationship.

People usually look for the good in others first if they themselves are good. NPS individuals present themselves very well. Being attracted to and bonding with what we believe is good happens. God warns us in our belly—our gut feeling, our intuition—of a threat. There is no evidence. The only proof of the threat is our gut. We play a part in the dysfunctional connection if and when we ignore God's gift of intuition (our belly, or gut feeling), other clues, or advice from those who have traveled this path. Never ignore the obvious or seek a lie for comfort because the truth hurts.

Often I think about David in the Bible. He was chosen by God to be the next king of Israel. He wasn't looking for that position; he was happy tending his father's sheep. David loved his family, God, and his king, Saul. God gave David success in everything that he did because of this.

After David defeated Goliath, the champion of the Philistines, Saul wanted to keep David in his service until one day, the people sang a song that praised David! Shortly after that, the jealous king forced David to become a fugitive because Saul repeatedly tried to kill him. Saul would fly into a rage and try to capture and kill David, David would profess his love and loyalty to the king, and then Saul would apologize with tears in his eyes. And the cycle would repeat itself! This went on for years!

David stayed away from Saul because the condition of that man warranted danger no matter what he said tearfully. This wasn't unforgiveness or revenge; it was proactive life preservation. David had to pray, run, and find trustworthy support. The king's son was his best friend. Jonathan was that person.

> The prudent see danger and take refuge, but
> the simple keep going and suffer for it. (Proverbs
> 27:12)

The best course in any relationship is to proceed with wisdom and watch as well as pray. Do not ignore any red flags or advertise them. If you feel a desperate need to ignore red flags, that is a signal that something needs attention and correcting within yourself. Analyze your current position and proceed with wisdom.

CHAPTER 2

Your Position and Decisions

WHEN PEOPLE WE love harm us in ambiguous ways, the unspoken mixed messages are confusing. It is not uncommon to look within oneself for a cause. Women especially search for the area of failure to correct themselves and win back love. We wonder if we are to blame. Women worry about their looks, sexual prowess, submissiveness, or any traditional or cultural excuse they believe warrants mistreatment. They may think that if they correct some area of a possible failure, the mistreatment will stop.

Men can also worry about their looks or sexual prowess. (I do not think they do as much as women because society doesn't push those issues strongly toward men.) Men may believe that they are not successful, strong, financially secure, or romantic enough!

Siblings may feel like failures as children if they have not achieved enough or sacrificed enough to prove gratitude to their parents or caregivers!

The list of reasoning and blame is endless in all kinds of situations. The bottom line is that covert, or obvious, abuse is happening, and NPS abuse is usually very covert. The target feels the harm but cannot initially put their finger on it.

Toxic people are experts fluent in blame shifting, manipulation, lying, and denial. They do not want to own their harmful behavior.

Targets, the people NPS individuals look for a connection with, usually feel shame because they are attached to someone they discover is despicable, but they cannot readily prove or resolve the ambiguous danger and also have difficulty detaching. They do not understand how to navigate themselves in this dense fog of a relationship or clearly understand or explain what's wrong. We must understand our position in the relationship and make some decisions.

Knowing where you are internally as a person is even more important than any other information regarding recovery from toxic relationships. You may be the mountain that needs moving to get yourself out of this maze. Our internal condition draws us to some situations. I am amazed at the things that I didn't desire anymore in certain areas of my life when I dealt with some of my own nagging issues. Our personal issues may attract us to and bond us to NPS characters. It is paramount that we look within, focus on ourselves, and get personal—not relationship—help first. This way, we can unhook ourselves and learn to stay unhooked.

In the mall, on each level, is a map. The map is usually in some central area of each level. For example, a mall map may be located on the side of each escalator entrance. The map will have a marker, usually a red arrow, that reads, You Are Here!

From the exact location where you are reading, the map has a layout of everything around that area. Look around you, and you will find your way through each level from your exact standing point.

You also must know what you want. You may be looking for some particular store, the food court, restrooms, seating, or the exits. What do you want? Is it available in this mall at all? Now you can make better choices. If what you want is not even in that mall, you will never find it there, and you can stop looking and leave. Take your search elsewhere. Apply this to your situation. Unless you are kidnapped or in mortal danger, decide what you can change within and without that will change things for you.

> I call heaven and earth to record this day against you, that I have set before you life and death, blessing and cursing: therefore choose life, that both thou and thy seed may live. (Deuteronomy 30:19 KJV)

Moses was declaring the blessing and freedom to choose to serve God or not. He also made it clear that *there are two types of choices: choices that bless us and choices that curse us*. He suggested that we make blessed, life-giving choices. This blesses us personally and others, especially our families. We must make choices.

No one is born with a gift for making flawless choices. We learn from our experiences and those of others. I think everyone, even the NPS individual, is trying to choose what is best for them. Humans are designed for life, and what constitutes the quality of each life are the choices we make.

One of my favorite books is by Dr. Seuss, *Oh, the Places You'll Go*. The two first pages speak to my heart. They read,

> Congratulations! Today is your day. You're off to Great Places! You're off and away! You have brains in your head. You have feet in your shoes. You can steer yourself in any direction you choose.
>
> You're on your own. And you know what you know. And YOU are the guy who'll decide where to go. (Dr. Seuss, *Oh, the Places You'll Go*)

Most people have some control over their position in life. Our choices for whatever we have in life, especially relationships, began with an idea of what good we intended for ourselves or even others. The state of our personal development will guide us in how we pick and choose. This is not a put-down or a declaration of superiority; it is a beneficial statement that encourages us to check ourselves.

If we consistently successfully make good decisions, that is a valuable skill! Most of us try to consistently make good decisions and find that some were just wishful thinking. Others consistently make poor choices. The good news is that wherever we are in our decision-making skills and personal development, we can change and improve! Just look at your mall map and figure out your position and where you need or want to be.

Decisions begin in our minds. Our minds are complex and contain our behavior patterns, reasoning, emotions, data, information, beliefs, desires, preferences, experiences, attitude, and whatever skills we have acquired. People can be highly functional or function very low.

Genetic and pathological factors affect our brains also. The brain is God's masterpiece in all creatures; it regulates and manages life.

Sin and righteousness affect the behavior of everyone. Some people have disorders and conditions that affect their behavior. Behavior is what affects humankind and communities everywhere!

I think it is worth repeating that understanding oneself and then taking responsibility for ourselves is the key to unhooking from the NPS snare and finding good relationships. Most of what hooks people firmly in an NPS relationship is a need for a fulfillment in love, value, or something else that the NPS cannot supply, but we hope they can because we haven't or don't know how to meet our own needs.

Validation is just the beginning of freedom and healing from the emotional turmoil that develops in these highly toxic, addictive relationships.

Knowing the truth does not require arguments and pleading with your NPS partner. Just accept the facts and help yourself; you cannot change them. Remember your last plane ride. The flight attendant said, "Put your own oxygen mask on first if the cabin loses pressure!"

Some toxic people, or NPS persons, are permanent members of your family; or they are durable associates: spouses, relatives, siblings, parents, neighbors, employers, community, authorities, among others. We cannot change them. These people are part of our lives, and we have to learn how to live regardless of them. We do have the power to change ourselves, and then our lives will change.

> Do not conform any longer to the pattern
> of this world, but be transformed by the renew-
> ing of your mind. Then you will be able to test
> and approve what God's will is- his good, pleas-
> ing and perfect will. (Romans 12:2 NIV)

Our minds have to transform so that we can have better lives instead of grieving and striving to change the NPS individual that we love. We do not have to hate, mistreat, or malign anyone. Once we change how they fit into our lives, our lives will change—*forever*! This is the key to your freedom, recovery, and future.

CHAPTER 3

Awareness

*What we don't know can harm us. What we do
know can help us. Wisdom is learning to use information in a beneficial, correct, and relevant way.*

*Wisdom will save you from the ways of wicked
men, from men whose words are perverse,
who leave the straight paths to walk in dark
ways, who delight in doing wrong and rejoice
in the perverseness of evil, whose paths are
crooked and who are devious in their ways.*
—Proverbs 2:12–15 NIV

*Call to me and I will answer you and tell you
great and unsearchable things you do not know.*
—Jeremiah 33:3

Dᴀᴛᴀ ɪs ᴇᴠᴇʀʏᴡʜᴇʀᴇ. In our environment, millions of facts are
everywhere all the time about everything in this world. We collect
data that we believe is relevant to us and try to synthesize it into useful information to make wise choices in life.

*Awareness implies that we know now the data, the facts, and the
information that were always present but didn't notice for some reason!*

Something happened that brought them to our attention! Now we understand what we did not notice that was present all along. For example, when we go to school, we are taught math. Math is always present in different forms everywhere. We initially do not understand it, although it affects our lives. Math takes foundational data about digits 0–9, and depending on what you use math for, you can bake a really good cake or build an empire! Math is the numerical recipe of all matter that constitutes what is! Chemistry is the math that explains matter.

When we see or feel data, it may not be relevant because we do not understand what is happening. It does not appear with directions, so we can easily ignore it. We get a handle on data when something happens that connects the dots, and then we have information! After we get information, if we use it correctly, we have wisdom! Other people's wisdom is handy too.

Everyone has experiences, failures, and suffering that they have learned from. Now they use and share those valuable lessons and information with others to help them succeed.

> Praise be to the God and Father of our Lord Jesus Christ, the Father of compassion and the God of all comfort, who comforts us in all our troubles, so that we comfort those in any trouble with the comfort we ourselves have received from God. And our hope for you is firm, because we know that just as you share in our sufferings, so also you share in our comfort. (2 Corinthians 1:3–4, 1:7 NIV)

This is why it is important to seek help in acquiring wisdom from those who understand. We are taught that professionals, those with academic degrees, understand completely. After all, they do have great achievements in college. The higher the degree in studies, the more we believe we can trust their understanding of a matter to guide us through.

Some guides must be indigenous to the land to be most helpful to those in need. If I were in a jungle and had to choose between someone with a PhD in jungles and a native who successfully lives in that terrain, the native would be my first choice for a guide. Both people have expert knowledge to offer, but the one who has the most actual living experience (surviving and navigating that terrain) is the most helpful, in my opinion. Combining both the academic and the experienced is optimal.

The indigenous survivors do not just know about the scorpion stings; they have also been stung. They understand how it feels and know how to stop the poison! They may not be able to academically label the full spectrum of native species or have credentials from an accredited university to prove what they know; but they have encountered the scorpion's stings, survived them, and can help others do the same.

I am not suggesting that you do not get professional help once you are aware of your need. I am saying, "Shop wisely!" Everyone does not understand the twisted nature of NPS relationships. I have met professionals swayed by the charm of an NPS individual and lured into the same web that their clients came to for help with escaping. Cookie-cutter therapy or counseling will not help NPS targets!

People in the midst of NPS relationships, especially for the first time, have difficulty understanding or explaining their experience. It is difficult to confirm and resolve because you wonder, *What's happening?* You appear confused because it is confusing. Awareness—that is, a recognition of an NPS person and their behavior—helps confirm what's happening. After you are sure, obtaining help is in order. Help is available, and God is your biggest, most-powerful advocate besides yourself.

> For I am the LORD, your God, who takes
> hold of your right hand and says to you, Do not
> fear; I will help you. (Isaiah 41:13 NIV)

What's happening?

Everything begins somewhere. In the story *Lord of the Rings*, by Tolkien, it all began with the forging of the great rings… One ring was forged to rule them all: the Ring of Power!

Each ring was a gift that seemed to provide what each race wanted most, but a controlling power connected every ring to one master—the Ring of Power. This movie is a fabulous journey through Middle Earth, demonstrating the devastation possible with diabolical manipulation. I appreciate the story because the evil had to be destroyed where it was created.

Understanding how NPS characters operate will help us with awareness, and then we can deal with the root causes within ourselves that keep us attracted and hooked to them.

Understanding the situation does not remove evil or dysfunction from the world or our lives. We can learn to manage in our lives what we can identify that is affecting our lives.

Narcissistic-personality-syndrome (NPS) relationship cycles remind me of washing-machine cycles: they are predictable and sometimes immediately recognizable. *These are the NPS relationship cycles*: (1) idealizing, (2) love-flooding, (3) supplying, (4) devaluing and detaching, and finally, (5) discarding.

Just as washing machines have cycles (prewash, wash, spin, rinse, final spin, and then stop [and this is a whole cycle]), so do NPS relationships!

Sometimes the same cycles have different intensities, similar to washing machines: normal, gentle, and heavy cycles. What identifies the intensity of each cycle are the changes in temperature, agitation, and the duration of the entire process.

It is the same with an NPS relationship. The order or the phase of the cycle remains the same. It all begins with idealization.

Idealizing phase

Predator and prey are interesting positions. Predators have preferences, and prey prefer to survive them. I've never seen a lion pounce on a fig tree or jump in the lake to catch fish when they are hungry. They like wildebeest and other hoofed animals, like gazelles or zebras.

Targets of the NPS individual are usually chosen because of some quality that they possess that supports the NPS individual's needs. Idealization is when someone has a strong belief and expectation that another person (or situation) is the optimum choice for meeting one's personal needs.

Whatever meets the NPS individual's needs is called a supply. They have different needs, and no one can fill their bottomless pit. It is really sad; but, truthfully, they are empty people. Temporary distractions from that emptiness are the bane of both the NPS individual's and the target's lives.

It is a difficult situation because the target contributes to the dysfunctional dance. They crave something also. They want fulfillment, belonging, love, and security. It is a Venus-flytrap situation. These two are drawn to each other like a magnet and a paper clip. They intuitively feel the connection very strongly. The NPS individual wants to absorb the qualities they admire in their target. The target is exhilarated by the NPS attraction. The idea of what they each hope to extract from the other pulls them together in an unspoken transaction.

The trophy of the NPS individual is the fulfillment of narcissistic supply (which may include feelings of grandeur or importance, acquisition, power, admiration of others, etc.).

The trophy of the target is a secure relationship that fulfills personal-love, self-worth, and self-care deficits.

Targets are the queen or king on the throne of the other's life for a short while, and this love scene is very exciting and addictive. Even more addictive is the coming drama as the idealization unfolds.

The NPS individual is not in love; they are mimicking love. Neither are they evil geniuses plotting the whole event. Mimicking comes naturally with their condition. They are not thinking about it any more than a scorpion thinks about the poison in its tail. It naturally strikes under certain conditions, and so do they!

Oxford Languages defines drama *as an exciting emotional or unexpected series of events or circumstances. This is the nature of the idealization phase.* Both the NPS individual and the target are on a high of drama infused with ideas of each other that hopefully will supply their personal needs. Both people have a glorious expectation that is erroneous, and the target usually feels it first but ignores the red flag and proceeds anyway because it feels wonderful. What a terrible transaction!

Love-flooding phase

This phase immediately follows idealization. The NPS is smitten with you (i.e., their catch). Like a hunter with a trophy they take pictures of because no one will believe what was caught, the great hunter parades you in front of everyone to bolster their ego and yours. They, of course, never admit that's the real reason—if they even think about it. Remember, this behavior is automatic and natural for them. They are not really trying to mastermind it.

Love-flooding is magical for them too because it is spontaneous. You are admired, praised, and flooded with a tidal wave of romance and pleasure. It's the equivalent of drug addiction. Soon they'll need more, and you will need more as the flood continues. Intense affection, attention, and fast-paced joyous companionship, romance, involvement, and other enjoyable actions ensue. A cocoon is forming around you, but a butterfly is not coming out. (Trust me.)

They pour out in abundance public and private compliments, declarations of love, and commitment innuendos or promises. Statements ensuring support and importance are constantly being given. You both are really enjoying yourselves and not considering the cost. You both are amazed that you have each other.

This phase is also called *love bombing* because it is explosive and dynamic. All this powerful pleasure within a small cocoon of ecstasy will soon be revealed for what it really is. Instead of a beautiful butterfly emerging from a cocoon, Dracula comes out, disguised as a butterfly! And he's almost finished sucking the life out of you.

The smart vampires make your life-draining experience very pleasurable so that you sit still until they have completely drained you—literally! You sense your life being sucked away, but it feels so good that you deny or ignore the red flags.

Remember the movie *Interview with the Vampire*? There was a scene where two handsome vampires dressed up in the opera and seduced a beautiful lusty woman. As they drank every drop of her blood, they caressed her. Her last dying sentence was "Does your friend kiss as deeply as you?" She groaned with pleasure as she passed away. They left her dead body slumped over the chair and went out to consider their next victim. I'm not into vampire movies anymore. That scene made me think about the nature of some predators. By the way, in all fairness, women can be predators also.

Keep this in mind: the whole situation is addictive, very addictive. I am not going to sugarcoat anything as far as romance is concerned. If you are sexually involved with your NPS partner, it bonds you to them even more and not the other way around. They are not bonding. You are. They are consuming.

By now you recognize or are aware that you are stuck on the web of the spider! Do not be ashamed or go into denial. You may be enjoying the love flood, but the flood does stop. It does not usually happen abruptly. It dries up incrementally—guaranteed!

Just in case you didn't notice, most of your love floods are very public. A captive audience is necessary for the remaining cycles of the NPS drama. Later you will find out that the love flood was not only for you but also to groom the audience. Each audience member will find out their part in this drama later in your dilemma.

> A malicious man disguises himself with his
> lips, but in his heart he harbors deceit. Though
> his speech is charming, do not believe him, for
> seven abominations fill his heart. His malice

may be concealed by deception, but his wicked-ness will be exposed in the assembly. (Proverbs 26:24–26 NIV)

Supplying phase

The insatiable nature of NPS characters is because they are per-petually empty. The bottomless pit in their being cannot be filled by anyone or anything, so they must keep a flow moving through their lives to feel alive.

NPS individuals are anxious and preoccupied with a flow of supply! They do not call it a supply, but that is what keeps them going. Consistent hunting for whatever they lack is the draining stream under the calm surface of their lives. Everything they acquire has a very limited shelf life for them. It flows right out of them slowly or rapidly without fail. Only God can truly fill the void in their lives. He does save those who believe in Him, but they still struggle with the nature of their condition in relationships. The sad cycle for both the target and the NPS continues. We cannot fill them! They cannot fulfill us!

The dynamics of feeding (i.e., how they use you up) and supply (i.e., what they get out of the situation that supports them) is very twisted.

Remember the rush that both get initially! They approach you wide-eyed, turned on, and excited to connect, flooding you with love, possibilities, and compliments. You both feel so alive! The rush is unbelievable. This is why some people get out in the later end of this situation instead of the beginning and why they crave it again. It is similar to drug addiction. Understanding this can help one focus on correct reasoning and self-control.

They are very excited for all the expectations that seem promis-ing initially. You are bonding to all of this, and they are consuming it all. NPS individuals are only hungry for supply.

Their needs may not be what you imagine. Whatever they want to acquire may only make sense to them. For example, you may have some quality that they can attach to and, by association, extend that quality to themselves. Popularity, power, prestige, or access to various social or organizational avenues are examples of qualities in you that they can attach to. If you lack prestige, your lower position can benefit them because they are being honorable or are getting a sidekick. Any idea of what you represent in their life that magnifies their ego can be their supply.

You may not even be who they really want. It can be someone in close proximity to you that they can only get to if they are with you. You may still raise the question "Why didn't they go directly to that person and try to win them over?" Well, part of their behavior is to compulsively consume what they can as the main course is being prepared. As they lavish enviable behaviors on you, the true target has the front-seat opportunity to enjoy some stellar curb appeal.

A silent advertisement campaign is actively projected onto the true target. This is a form of triangulation. A tactic that pits actual or implied suitors against one another, jealousy and envy keep everyone hungry for the prize—the NPS individual! This comes naturally to them and is automatic, like all of their other behaviors. Triangulation makes them appear to be in demand.

Awareness is a very difficult part of mitigating toxic relationships because some people feel ashamed, stupid, weak, or embarrassed that they are in such a mess. Do not try to save face! Learn and move forward with these valuable lessons in your life belt. As far as being down on yourself is concerned, stop! Admirable qualities attract these people first. Strong, intelligent, successful, beautiful, and talented people supply them. Those who are frail, poor, ruined, unattractive, or ignorant supply them also. Everything goes! Remember, the NPS individual has something in them that needs filling. Helping the low, destitute person or even marrying or wooing the undesirable person makes them look like a hero. This is supply! How? It will attract the most desirable in the audience. They are now admired because they appear to be virtuous, empathetic, and heroic.

NPS individuals are very talented performers and perform very publicly to captivate an audience and sometimes build a fan base. These people are everyone around you, especially those closest to you. This builds up reserves of possibilities for them and their endless need for supply. It's a nice package for them and works against you. People begin to envy what they think you have.

When experiencing these things, the target usually has a gut feeling that something is wrong. Prayer and introspection can help put things into the correct perspective eventually. Watch and pray!

Jesus said to look at the fruit that a tree possesses, and that will reveal the condition of the tree, whether it is good or bad. The fruit also determines how trees are labeled. For example, apple trees are called that because they produce apples. No one looks at an apple tree and calls it anything else with fruit hanging on it. Some people look at the fruit on others and ignore it because they consider that judging or condemning, but Jesus said to look.

> You can identify them by their fruit, that is, by the way they act. Can you pick grapes from thorn bushes, or figs from thistles? A good tree produces good fruit, and a bad tree produces bad fruit. A good tree can't produce bad fruit, and a bad tree can't produce good fruit. So every tree that does not produce good fruit is chopped down and thrown into the fire. *Yes, just as you can identify a tree by its fruit, so you can identify people by their actions.* (Matthew 7:16–20 NLT; emphasis added)

What is confusing about these toxic relationships is that the presentation is so good. You see it, and everyone else sees it and wants it. And that supplies the NPS individual and threatens you! You can feel the tiny unraveling of that awesome connection as they begin their covert ambiguous departure.

If you begin to flake apart, trying to understand all the harm you feel but cannot prove, you give them supply. They have broken you; and they happily feed on that. The stronger, better, and more successful you are, the more pleasure they get from your demise. Now you fear that what your gut is telling you is true. They are either on their way out or being unfaithful, maybe both.

That fear shows up in your health. You are depressed, under- or overeating, or nervous every time they do anything or go anywhere. Your sleep is all messed up; you may go from short periods of deep sleep and long waking hours or the opposite—sleeping all the time, staying awake for short hours, or experiencing insomnia. Thinking becomes stressful. They are enjoying this. If they can behave extremely badly right under your nose, that really supplies them because now they have an adventure to enjoy. It can get pretty horrible.

All your misery is supplying them, and then something else happens. They begin to parade the wreck of a person you are becoming with fake concern and secret complaints to the audience (those around you and those closest to you). A continuing performance of excellent character continues in public. All of this confusion is supply. *Give them nothing!* Take your concerns to God and pray for strength to acknowledge the truth about your situation. Pray for peace, wisdom, help, and direction because more is to come in the next cycle.

The next phase will begin as soon as they are completely sure they have secured new supply. This happens quickly because they have been grooming, triangulating, and selling themselves to people all along and giving them opportunities to think about all the good they hope to get out of them, the faux wonderful person.

The new target will get exactly what you got—cyclical narcissistic relationship cycling! Your addiction to this person manifests in withdrawal-type symptoms that begin the minute your intuition receives the signal that it is truly over, even if they are still around and denying that they want to leave. Your body will give you information because that gift of intuition is picking up on the truth. Honestly, they like straddling the fence for as long as possible because their fear is having no supply or less than they are used to.

Devaluing-and-detaching phase

The toxic person has to keep their mask intact so that others they've targeted do not run for cover if their true nature is revealed. They also need to figure out how to transition away from you while still feeding on you.

They understand that what they are doing is wrong, but they also believe some of the lies about themselves that they present to others. To keep up the delusion about themselves in front of themselves and others, they create chaos to justify what behaviors pour out of them next.

They can only hold their bad behavior in for so long because this is the true fruit that they bear. It is becoming more difficult for them to keep up their honorable show. Baiting you into drama in private and in public is also a show for others to solicit pity and support from them. Any drama they can bait out of you is false evidence for a court you were not aware that you were in. *This invisible court is the audience,* who will begin to agree with the NPS individual that something is wrong with you and that it is amazing that they have stayed with you. Soon the NPS individual will have license to pour out contempt and more harm publicly on you with approval from the audience. Soon the person/s they are moving toward will not feel bad about displacing you once they realize they have a place. The shift is gradual and damaging. They relish in the damages. This is the reason toxic people are called energy vampires: the drama and deception are draining.

Another behavior during this phase may be off-putting. They may show you more affection to distract you, and you can feel the gap. You are now a proxy for what they want to give someone else. You become the understudy for the new supply, so they practice with you. And this is painful because you cannot prove what your gut is telling you.

Do not ignore your gut! Do not forget this: the new target is a target, and they are being groomed to receive the same experience you are now in. The NPS individual is the same and repeating the same behavior with someone new! I mentioned this because the temptation to compete will be present. Do not compete for them. It is still a loss.

> As a dog returns to its vomit, so a fool repeats his folly. (Proverbs 26:11)

Criticizing is part of devaluation. Nothing about you is good enough anymore. Every imaginable and unimaginable flaw will be cast on you. With the same intensity that they love-bombed you, they will devalue you if they are sure there is new supply intact. Occasionally, some will completely sever ties abruptly without any warning. Some will try to enjoy breaking you on their way out no matter how long that takes. This is why it is critical that you deal with yourself before you focus too much on the relationship as soon as you are sure of your situation. You will need to keep going forward once you start going.

I think it was Winston Churchill who stated, "If you're going through hell, keep going [until you are out]!"

If the NPS individual is someone permanently part of your life—like a parent, sibling, child, employer, or relative—self-management and self-care will help you set up appropriate boundaries. This is for your own protection and well-being, and there is nothing wrong with that. Some people believe that this is wrong for various reasons, but it is not wrong to protect yourself from harmful people.

If you are dating, engaged to, or married to an NPS individual, you will need to consider the next steps without threatening them. They are who they are, and threats do not change them and will not help you. Sometimes a clever tactic for them is to revert back to love flooding to either rehook you or harm you more until they replace you.

They want a new stream of supply to feed on. The relationship is ending, and no matter how long someone manages to prolong this or dwell in denial, the NPS individual is moving on even if they are chewing their way out through you and your resources. Draining resources and ruining others' credit are also easy ways to make the targets vulnerable or stuck in the mud. Guard and monitor your resources, identity, accounts, and devices for malicious activity.

> The end of a matter is better than its beginning, and patience is better than pride. Do not be quickly provoked in your spirit, for anger resides in the lap of fools. (Ecclesiastes 7:8–9 NIV)

Discarding phase

This is the last phase. This phase is excruciating. Being discarded is so painful. No one wants to get dumped, broken-up with, or left. Being discarded from a narcissistic relationship is traumatic because of the dramatic nature of the entire relationship.

Constant criticism, open discontent, complaints, and comparisons will get heavy at times. They are building a fortress in their minds to justify leaving for no real reason. The dream come true has turned into a twilight zone! We are almost out. Keep going forward.

The "Awareness" section of the book is the most extensive and should be read prayerfully and patiently because it is difficult information for hurting hearts. It is not exhaustive but contains enough to identify whether or not you are in a NPS relationship. We must be aware of the narcissistic-personality-syndrome (NPS) relationship (the cycles). We must be aware of the person/s with this condition (the approach and our attraction and gut warnings). More importantly, we must be aware of ourselves (our neediness, emptiness, or boredom). The shock, anger, and betrayal during the discarding can send one reeling into a self-destructive course, but it doesn't have to. *God will help you. Trust in Him and do good.*

Exiting will prove the most dramatic part of the relationship because of how bonded we are to our NPS partner. Our needs bonded us to them like superglue. Their needs attached them to us like a vampire. When all the life is sucked out, they fly off into the night. To them, this is just survival.

The finality of it, the damages, the tumultuous memories, the beautiful memories, the breach of trust in loved ones and friends who did not understand how they got sucked into this, and the disappointing counselors who meant well but may not understand make looking into the future grim. Do not despair. Healing will come, and a better future is available.

Now we will walk through the end. The lack of closure disturbs people the most—when we are asking why, how, when, what, and who and get nothing. They keep going, and you are trying to get unstuck in so many ways. You want answers. You want to find the cause and effect so maybe you can fix things and get back to a wonderful life, like the one you had at the beginning. That smoke screen is gone. They are finished unless they can entertain themselves by hurting you some more. Sometimes they even get their new target/s to participate in the mistreatment. The new target believes the NPS individual's complaints about you and also have been pumped up with comparisons. They cook better; make more money; look better; are stronger and sexier; etc. The list can be endless if the new target needs convincing to buy into the relationship. The new target does not know that they are going to get what you got or worse!

The NPS relationship cycles endure just like the seasons of the year—spring, summer, fall, and winter—and there is nothing anyone can do about that.

Warning the new target will not help them or you. They are high on love flooding, just like you were!

The new target will also arrive at the discarding phase eventually. It is important for the NPS to involve the new target in mistreating you now because when they get to this phase with them, it will be thrown up into their faces! "Don't call me evil! You didn't have a problem with me when…," they'll exclaim.

Remember the scripture Ecclesiastes 7:8–9: "Pause, do not be provoked, grieve and let God help you through this." Do not fight the new target, and do not engage or fight with the NPS individual. Do not entertain yourself by imagining the worst for them. Thank God that you now understand what happened in your life. Now you have knowledge and wisdom to help you in the future. Understanding and recognizing these things helps you make better future decisions and protect yourself. You may even help someone else with what you've learned—that is, if they listen and learn.

God will wipe the tears from your eyes and give you a new better life. Pray for the NPS individual and the next target and understand that this and forgiveness are the most powerful things you can do to heal and move forward in your life.

God is with you, loving you and helping you every day.

Repeat the affirmation above to yourself but personalize it!

God is with me, loving me and helping me every day! Hallelujah! Thank you, *Lord*.

CHAPTER 4

Who Are You?

Understanding who we are and how that contributes to our experience is very important. The targets of narcissistic-personality-syndrome (NPS) and other toxic relationships play a part in the web they get stuck in.

We contribute to the toxic dance with corresponding dance steps. If you are dancing with someone, you must do the same dance; otherwise, you are tripping over each other. Someone leads in the waltz, and the other follows. If they are waltzing and you're doing the Electric Slide, you are not dancing together. The steps are different, and the music is different. These differences clash. To continue trying to simultaneously hang on to two different dances that require opposite genres of music is ridiculous and tremendously cumbersome. Either we are dancing together, or we are not. Targets are dancing with the NPS individuals. The dance stops when we decide to change our moves.

Awareness of both sides of this situation can help us put on the brakes and change our moves. Now we must look at ourselves.

What we want interferes with our reasoning at times. Culture, religion, politics, society, our life experiences, our personality, others' personalities, our mental and emotional condition, how we attach and detach in relationships, sexuality, education, etc. affect our behavior.

The average healthy person possesses the ability to understand and meet their own basic needs. We understand how to ask for help when we need it. We try to learn skills to help meet our own needs. Food, clothing, shelter, love, faith, and belonging seem to make for a satisfactory life. Personal power and achievement, contributions, and legacy take life up a notch.

Sharing all of these wonderful things with someone special in an intimate, loving relationship can be extremely rewarding. It's a beautiful concept to pursue. Targets must not only be aware of what they want but also of who they are. It is also beneficial to be aware of how we possibly got to where we are now.

We fit into the toxic dance when our wants and needs correspond with what the NPS individual presents to us, and we believe their cha-rade. We believe it because something in us makes it believable. The truth is that we have similar cycles as they, but for different reasons and durations, this affects our decisions.

We idealize. This is because we are hungry to belong in an ideal situation. We already have an idea of the NPS individual when we encounter them. The erroneous idea that being chosen by anyone is a relationship privilege, especially for women, is the beginning of our problems. This belief in the wrong frame of mind is also a problem for men.

The desire to have certain needs met within ourselves begins a snow squall of wishful thinking because we are either not meeting our own needs or starved for something missing in our lives. People who have not developed personal self-care skills or personal responsibility may believe that love is someone else providing our needs. The NPS individual appears to be that provider! Just as snow squalls are sudden and intense with little or no visibility, the ideas and wishes that we have for our possible love connection are blinding us when we connect to our NPS partner. The safe thing to do in a snow squall is to pull over until it dissipates or proceed slowly and cautiously.

During idealization, a target who is suffering from any type of low-self-concept issues may instantly begin selling themselves. "Choose me, choose me!" cries our behavior!

The righteous choose their friends carefully,
but the way of the wicked leads them astray.
(Proverbs 12:26 NIV)

If we are happier to be chosen than we are to choose some good-quality relationship, this is a warning that we need to stop and work on ourselves. God wants us to make good choices. If we do not know how, we can pray for wisdom, and He will teach us. This passage (Proverbs 12:26) instructs us to be careful when choosing friends because wicked people will lead us astray. The NPS relationship is deceitful and not a healthy relationship. Be careful. We may project all our ideas onto someone who targeted us and disappoint ourselves because of being anxious to connect.

Most people, once out of this situation, can identify their mistakes and the times that they ignored the red flags. The NPS individual knows what most people want—that is, love, support, belonging, admiration, power, excitement, faithfulness, acceptance, and commitment.

Another interesting thing that happens when we encounter this possible connection is a surge of coincidences! This is called *mirroring behavior*. It appears that we are literally alike and extremely compatible. If the NPS individual has been observing us for a while or quietly listening to us around others, they can put together quite a convincing show of compatibility. Whatever we do not give them, they will try to fish out of us and then mirror us. This is instant fake compatibility.

Our idea of them appears to come to life as they morph into what they've learned about us. This Trojan horse is how they get into our lives. They hide inside our idea of what we want, and then the real them comes out once they are firmly in place in our lives.

In the story of Troy, the enemy could not get through the great walls that protected the city. So they built a beautiful huge horse, and the army hid inside it. Troy's citizens marveled at this glorious gift that appeared at the gates. They celebrated this gift from the gods. At night, when the drunken celebration was over, the army came out of the horse and destroyed the city.

Your intuition will kick in at some point during the beginning of the relationship. Do not ignore it. God is trying to tell you something!

> I will instruct you and teach you in the way
> you should go; I will counsel you and watch over
> you. (Psalm 32:8 NIV)

If there is a connection, the next phase for the target will be feeding and supplying, the same as the NPS individual but for different reasons. In the beginning, there seems to be a perfect match (whatever that represents for us). Our idea is perfect bliss. Thoughts and wishes of sharing, bonding, growing closer, being inseparable, and experiencing the best relationship ever excite us. The entire scenario blossoms in a spectacular display that is very public. It appears that we are getting our wish, and it looks promising.

In the *feeding-and-supplying phase*, we are absorbing everything that we believe—that is, idealizing this relationship to fulfill ourselves. It is so wonderful, and everyone is watching, which adds to the joy for us and secretly comes in handy for the NPS individual also. We anxiously provide our friends and family with the amazing details and coincidences that led up to this dream come true. We are glowing and happy, some people are happy for us, and others are jealous (this is kinda our supply too).

If you are the person chosen after they got out of a "bad" relationship with someone else who is "inferior" to you, you are feasting. This lifts your confidence if you are low on it. You do not know it, but this is supplying the NPS because the former target is watching you replace them and hurting.

The NPS is getting supply, and so are you—for opposite reasons. It is in this position that the most ground is destroyed in your life because during all this sweet commotion, you are sharing deep secrets with your NPS confidant, sharing your resources, introducing them to those close to you in different areas of your life, and sharing the most meaningful things about yourself. The perpetrator has hit the jackpot because you believe that you have hit the jackpot! Here is where they build their arsenal for the shift that is soon to come: the devaluing-and-detaching phase. The greatest show on earth has an effect on you because you are the current supply, and the last discarded target is residual supply.

The *devaluing-and-detaching phase* is different for targets because instead of letting go of the NPS individual, they let go of people they believe will interfere with their bond to the NPS individual!

The NPS will complain at some point that jealous people are trying to separate or interfere with your relationship. Negative communication about others will progressively move your heart away from someone who recognizes the threat to you and is trying to help you. This can be anyone outside looking in with wisdom—a loved one, an associate, or even their former target. You do not know who to trust because everyone comes to the oasis for a drink in the desert, both predators and targets!

Other toxic people may envy you and try to pull the rug from underneath you to poach what they believe that you have. Someone else who wants you may try to disturb the relationship. The NPS individual is keenly aware of threats to their supply, and if there is competition they will love-flood you a little more to ensure your attachment to them.

As you begin detaching from your audience (i.e., those closest to you and those around you), the NPS individual is secretly bonding with them.

You have proven your undying love and commitment to the NPS, and now that you have let others go, you can fully focus on them. Then you notice the gap!

The adoration, admiration, and praise has dried up! You try to talk about the sudden deficit in your closeness, and they tell you that it's all in your head.

After they infiltrate every facet of your life and share even the most precious resources that you have, you cannot even find comfort. They make everything painful. Your favorite song hurts, and your spot in the park that cheers you up hurts. It also hurts when you go to your place of worship because they've captivated everyone there. You go to your family and friends and find out that they have been turned against you.

Now you are so alone, and in the coming days, all the fury of this mess will rapidly unfold. As you notice the damages and losses, you know that you need to get out but do not know how. What is worse is that something happened to you in this situation.

You have become addicted to this person and didn't realize it. You don't understand what that feels like until you try to leave. Because leaving begins in your mind, every time you think about leaving, you get physically ill.

Some targets find out that their money and credit are also used up. They have losses that they weren't even aware of before because they were enjoying and preoccupied with the ride.

Now you're mourning and grieving. You realize that your personal infrastructure has been damaged or destroyed. Faith, love, joy, trust, creativity, playfulness, vision, hope, contentment, and fellowship are in ruins (just to mention some) and need repairs badly.

There will be a period of intense manipulation and various tactics to destroy you and bolster the NPS individual up as you reach the final phase—discarding. They not only want to discard you; they also want your closest loved ones to discard you so that you are isolated, wiped out, and without hope for recovery. This is narcissistic-personality-syndrome (NPS) rage! When we discard, it begins with a desire to survive! It is not an evil need to destroy anyone, so discarding is different for us.

> The thief comes only to steal and kill and
> destroy; I have come that they may have life, and
> have it to the full. (John 10:10 NIV)

The Lord will help us.

Discarding is the final phase. The target does not devalue or detach the way the NPS individual does. The relationship is valuable to the target, so they want it to work out. This is where counseling, searching for resolutions for the flood of complaints and accusations from the NPS individual, and praying for a miracle and help ensue.

On top of all of this battling, there is the mysterious illness that suddenly flares up when you try to leave or accept that the whole relationship is false and over. It is a withdrawal symptom.

Only people who have experienced this truly understand you. If the NPS individual wooed them, do not trust them for help. They have been groomed to look at you as the problem. They cannot help you because they are also under the influence of narcissistic manipulation. You are discarding in your heart for protection, and you are grieving everything you hoped for from this person. The same can ring true of any relationships affected this way.

Arguing and bargaining will not help you. Telling this person that they need help because they have a narcissistic personality disorder will not help! They are done with you and do not think that they are wrong anyway. Crying, voicing suicidal thoughts, and expressing pain give them supply, increase their disrespect for you, and make them want to get away faster. If they respond with a little kindness, beware! Any recant of leaving or new display of love may be because they need to drain you some more while they find satisfactory resources elsewhere.

Sometimes the NPS individual wants two sources because each has something they value. For example, if you have money, they need that. If the other person is powerful in the community, they need that for access to that community. So you both are supplying. Awareness opens your eyes to the nature of what is happening now. Divine help is needed. God helps us move with wisdom toward deliverance from such circumstances.

> And the Lord shall deliver me from every evil work and preserve me unto His heavenly kingdom to whom be glory for ever and ever. Amen. (2 Timothy 4:18 KJV)

> Be strong and take heart, all you who hope in the Lord. (Psalm 31:24 NIV)

Some people pray for God to change the relationship back to the wonderful phase. He will not because that would be reenacting a lie. God does not lie. We must believe that there is healing and a better life. God will not control others for us. He does not control anyone to make them love Him! Your NPS loved one may be a believer, and God will move in their lives because of their wrongs, just like He does with everyone else. They know right from wrong. We do too. Remember this: God has given us power to be great. God has given us the power to be a recipient and source of His awesome love. God has also given us the ability to have a sound mind and do right.

At this point, resist the temptation to discard God because you are hurting. He is your powerful stronghold at this time of trouble. You can hold up in Him as long as it takes for you to heal and grow, and you'll emerge victorious! Hallelujah!

Good news!

Now that we have walked through the validation (i.e., understood the accuracy of our situation) and awareness (i.e., we recognize the fruits of our situation and ourselves), we can begin the journey to a better future.

God bless you!

CHAPTER 5

You've Got the Power!

Transforming and improving our lives is 100 percent possible! You may be clutching your broken heart right now, but get ready to be blessed. God is our greatest resource for change! He is on our side and guaranteeing us help if we want it. I must add this: God does not guarantee that we will understand or like how He helps, but He will and is helping. If we trust in the Lord and do good, we will notice His almighty hand doing His wonderful, mysterious work in our lives, and we can participate in the miracle by first trusting in Him. We also must be willing to do our part.

> Don't copy the behavior and customs of this world, but let God transform you into a new person by changing the way you think. Then you will learn to know God's will for you, which is good and pleasing and perfect. (Romans 12:2 NLT)

There is a period where you will feel like grieving is your new future. It is not, believe me. Better days are coming.

> "For I know the plans that I have for you," declares the Lord, "plans to prosper you and

not to harm you, plans to give you hope and a future." (Jeremiah 29:11 NIV)

Decide right now to accept that you are hurt but also that you will heal. Decide not to curl up and cease living. Decide not to spend the rest of your life hypervigilant and worrying about your NPS/toxic loved one or going no-contact with them! Decide to contact God, pull up the will to accept His help, and watch life get better. Decide to get off the complaining powwows where other targets repeatedly complain about what was done to them. Decide to stay focused on how great God is instead of your NPS ex! Decide to make these excellent decisions *right now*!

Read and repeat scriptures that strengthen you. Repeat thanking God for getting you out of your difficult situation (even before it happens). Repeat positive affirmations to reinforce awesome thinking. Repeat songs that lift you up and inspire you. Think on and repeat these things. This is meditation.

> Blessed is the man who does not walk in the counsel of the wicked or stand in the way of sinners or sit in the seat of mockers. But his delight is in the law of the LORD, and on His law he meditates day and night. He is like a tree planted by streams of water, which yields fruit in season and whose leaf does not wither. Whatever he does prospers. Not so the wicked! They are like the chaff that the wind blows away. Therefore the wicked will not stand in the judgment, nor sinners in the assembly of the righteous. For the LORD watches over the way of the righteous, but the way of the wicked will perish. (Psalm 1 NIV)

Our mind is the universe for us. It is our inner world. This is the environment we must cultivate to improve our quality of life.

Part of self-empowerment is taking responsibility for our thought life. It is not easy because of the old mental and attitudinal habits.

These must be replaced with excellent mental and attitudinal habits. God will help us, but we must decide that it's time to change and ask for His help. Our minds are powerful because God made them that way.

Pray and ask God for wisdom and understanding. Everyone has different NPS situations, and some are more damaging than others. It will take God's miraculous navigation and strength to get through and out of this. We can give God the reins of our lives, and God will hold them through us and help us begin the journey to abundant living, joy, peace, and deep healing. We will look forward to a better future and turn every loss, damage, hurt, insult, fear, abuse, and worry over to Him. The past is a history lesson to protect our future.

> For God has not given us a spirit of fear but
> of power and of love and of a sound-mind. (2
> Timothy 1:7 NKJV)

Just as your phone has built-in applications (apps) that enable certain services, so do we! Our built-in life apps are available for use on activation. Some will only work if we activate them, and others must automatically work to enable basic life functions. God has given us three built-in apps, but they need activation. *The first one is power.* Power is can-do ability or abilities!

> I can do all things through Christ who
> strengthens me. (Philippians 4:13)

When we make up our minds to transform and improve our lives, we are also on the path to learning excellent lessons and setting excellent boundaries. We discover that we are able to think better and choose better; therefore, we can live better. *Can-do! Power!* We do not have to understand everything at all times, but just choosing better allows us to feel in our hearts what is not for us.

Toxic relationships are harmful and sometimes dangerous, and as we activate power, a shift takes place. We begin to understand the areas in our lives that kept us hooked, and we begin to detangle and unhook ourselves with the help of the Lord. We take back power. The NPS individual feels the power drain from the situation. Because they need to drain you, they will immediately begin tactical behaviors to lasso you back in. Please continue to grow in personal power! God is with you, helping you every day.

Power is can-do, and these are some things we can do:

1. *We can pray.* God is present to help in trouble (Psalm 46:1). This means He is always available twenty-four hours daily. He will not gossip about your business or put you down for your struggles and shortcomings. Ask God for all the support that you need, and He will help you. The only thing God will not do is change someone into what you want them to be. He has given every human free will to decide how they want to believe, behave, or respond to Him. God does not force anyone to love or obey Him, so He is not changing people against their will to please us. When you pray, trust that God is helping you and your situation.

2. *We can learn about ourselves.* Taking time to understand yourself is powerful proactive behavior. If we are honest with ourselves, we may find that we become dependent and expect others to infuse our lives with what we do not even contribute to ourselves. Neediness and ignorance make up the love potion of dysfunctional relationships. Once we understand ourselves and take responsibility to learn how to meet our own needs in healthy ways and practice them, we stop settling and being attracted to toxic intimate relationships. We think about what we hope someone else would do for us, and then we care for ourselves. This doesn't mean that we are antisocial or needless. We just learn to have balance and responsibility. This can mean asking for help when we really need it. After all, no one is an expert at everything.

3. *We can set boundaries.* We learn to understand that it is right to set boundaries in all areas of life, especially with toxic people. Dr. Henry Cloud wrote an excellent book

about this called *Boundaries*. In this book, Cloud helps people understand how to draw lines between themselves and others to regain control of their lives. I highly recommend this book. It is a life changer! Boundaries are needed to keep life balanced. This is why road lines, fences, traffic lights, on-off switches, laws, and law enforcement (to name a few) are very important.

4. *We can say yes or no and know why!* Figure out why you allow or do not allow, accept or reject, and agree to or disagree to anything. Understand that you do not have to always get others to understand for your yeses and nos to be appropriate for you. Remember, toxic people only think about getting their way at all costs and really don't care about your wants, needs, or feelings. You must care about these yourself and decide when to negotiate and how to make decisions.

5. *We can improve ourselves.* The most wonderful project we can embark on is meaningful self-improvement. Resist the scourge of codependents—that is, managing and enabling other people to gain value and acceptance. Improve yourself. Be patient with yourself and expect no applause from anyone. Self-improvement is not an attention-seeking activity; it is a life-improvement behavior. You will discover that the world still has its issues, but life is good for you anyway.

6. *We can let go!* Letting go is releasing people, things, and situations that drain the life out of our lives! Gardeners prune back foliage to enable excellent production! Pruning makes the flowers more robust. The fruit and vegetables are bigger and more delicious, and the trees grow taller and more lush! Pruning improves us also. God prunes us so that we can be more productive.

7. *We can imagine!* Instead of using your imagination to fear, use it to visualize a wonderful life full of joy and great potential, because we have great potential! Even while you are still trying to get your life back in order, you can

imagine a better life. Without imagination you cannot recognize success. Imagine what you want that is actually in your sphere of control. Imagine a happy, peaceful, strong, content life. Imagine yourself *not* under the influence of toxic manipulation. Imagine yourself achieving goals that you gave up on because of your situation. Imagine yourself calmly facing your toxic loved one without fear, hate, hurt, or guilt because you unhooked yourself from their web. Imagine yourself trusting God to meet all your needs instead of hoping that the NPS individual you've been addicted to will. Imagine successful resolution of personal issues. *Imagine!*

8. *We can take courage!* Plant and cultivate courage in your life. Courage is the ability to do what you must even in the midst of dreading it. Throughout Scripture God commanded His people to take courage. God knew the only way to move out of failure and into success was to do what one must despite fear and anxiety. He also commanded His people *not to fear*, because it was easier to obey a command rather than a seminar. God's encouragement was that He is with us.

> This is My command—be strong and courageous! Do not be afraid or discouraged. For the LORD your God is with you wherever you go. (Joshua 1:9 NLT)

Fear is a control mechanism of toxic people. After the love-flood period, it is easy to become a romance junkie. Now, with God's help, we are aware of these things, depend on the *Lord* for true love, and do not try to extract perfect love from anyone. It also will take courage to heal, continue developing, thrive, love ourselves, and (after these) love others correctly.

CHAPTER 6

The Power of Love

THE SECOND APP is love. Love is a powerful force. Love moves God. Love moves people. Love has a powerful influence for good and evil wherever it abides. God's love for us resulted in a resolution to our unpayable sin debt—that is, salvation through Jesus Christ (John 3:16). Love makes people do beneficial things for themselves and others. Love is why different people master various arts, disciplines, and focuses and provides mankind with all sorts of benefits, solutions, products, and pleasures. Think about medical arts, technology, concepts, architecture, cuisine, agriculture, music, dance, perfume, airplanes, sports, and clothes. Millions of systems, solutions, organizations, and products exist because someone loved *something*!

On the negative side, love can also be a destructive force. The love of wickedness produces most of the harm and destruction suffered by mankind. Loving oneself to the complete detriment of others is narcissistic behavior. Loving any kind of sinful behavior damages oneself and others.

Love must be harnessed for good, and God has put the power of love within each human. We all have the capacity to receive and share love on some level. God leaves the decisions about how we harness our power of love up to us because He has given us free will.

Sin taints love. So many of the encounters with what we believe is love is usually just a feel-good substitute, similar to artificial sweetener. It's sweet, but it's not sugar.

> There is no fear in love; but perfect love
> casts out fear, because fear involves torment. But
> he who fears has not been made perfect in love.
> (1 John 4:18 KJV)

Fear and love do not go together, yet so many people avoid love because of fear. We do not want to be hurt when "in love." No one wants to lose what they love. Love done wrong turns into a threat. We are most vulnerable when we love. We are our strongest when we love.

Love is weaponized in toxic relationships, especially those involving narcissistic personality syndrome (NPS). Because we are designed to love, we find ourselves operating in it in some kind of way. We are either loving in a positive way, or we are using love destructively. Millions of people are ruined by love abuse. *Love abuse* is using love or love concepts to control, manipulate, pervert, molest, victimize, sexually abuse, harm, traffic, entrap or mentally, physically, or emotionally destroy or harm someone/others. Predators specialize in this.

To harness the positive power of love to heal ourselves, enjoy healthier relationships, and make wiser choices, we must first realize what love is not! If we engage in things that are misinterpreted as love, we harm ourselves with a misconception.

Love is not

1. romance—Oxford Languages defines romance as the excitement and mystery associated with love,
2. sex or sexual satisfaction,
3. someone you agree with all the time or someone who agrees with you all the time,
4. having fun all the time,
5. solely attraction,
6. drama.

Love is an enduring quality that is better than all these things. All these things are better with love but are not love.

People who are suffering from the effects of love misconceptions or love abuse usually are more anxious to connect to erroneous forms of love. They become romance addicts. They are in love until the excitement is gone. They only want the excitement or the drama. When these elements are gone, they are miserable. Sexual pleasure, for some, drives them to search for the ultimate sexual encounter. If they find it, for a short while, that is love for them—until they get bored.

A person who has never experienced sexual satisfaction may believe that a satisfactory sexual encounter with someone represents love. They may not understand that some people do not need to be in love to have sex. For them, it is just a pleasurable activity with no emotional attachment. Narcissistic people enjoy using sex not only for their own pleasure but also as weapons. They know that sex is perceived by some to represent love, and they use that misconception to their advantage.

Without creating a preachment about love, I will state a biblical fact: we will not receive the best that love has to offer outside of a relationship with God through Jesus Christ. Look at the things society is suffering from. It is clear that what we are missing is love God's way in our world. Again, I am not talking about romance and sexuality, just love.

To experience the power of love, we must receive God's love. People's love runs out for many reasons, but God's love never fails. This is true love security. Misconceptions about God's love can rob us of the power of connection to Him. God's love does not exist to do our bidding. It does not guarantee protection from the adversity and troubles present in this world. We will have trouble. Jesus said this, and He will help us. (Read John 16:33.)

God's never-ending love is an eternal, unconditional source of pure love that He has lavished on us! It gives us life, connection, and personal power. With God's love filling our hearts, we can have miraculous faith and endurance through this life! It creates wonderful potential for all of us. By accepting this love, God's love, we can heal from the damages caused by our own and others' behavior. Because it is perpetually flowing through us, we can learn to harness its presence to love ourselves and others correctly. We then become a source of love, not one who is needy, desperate, and hopeless. Knowing that God loves us may not extinguish all the pain of rejection and betrayal that we have experienced in relationships. It is a firm bedrock of personal infrastructure to survive these hurts. Even as survivors, we can still function properly with balance, love, and hope.

Nonnarcissistic loving of ourselves is self-care and fulfills our responsibility to ourselves. An NPS individual will approach a relationship like a spider. They will spin a web to catch someone, and like a spider, they will paralyze and wrap up their catch to suck the life out of them at will. This is not love.

Harnessing the power of love includes taking responsibility for oneself in a healthy, nondestructive way. We do not latch on to and leech the life out of others. When connected to God, our true love source, we develop a lifestyle of learning to meet our own needs correctly. Practicing this is self-care. We accept responsibility for ourselves. We do not try to manipulate and guilt-trip others into doing for us what we should learn how to and can do for ourselves.

Seeking others to infuse our lives with what only we and God can give gives opportunities to predator personalities. This is why learning and practicing self-care is so important.

Basic self-care skills will include physical hygiene, proper nutrition, exercise, proper rest, enriching activities, education, personal development, and some kind of work, chores, or duties (paid or volunteer). They include hobbies, creative expressions, and enjoying our own company. They also include careful social interactions with others, obtaining medical care and other services when necessary, personal safety practices, responsible communication, and spiritual faith. We develop the ability to ask for or seek help properly when necessary. We learn and practice assertive skills and boundaries. We love and take care of ourselves. People with disabilities, handicaps, and other conditions that need assistance are practicing self-care when they seek out, request, and accept appropriate services to help them manage caring for themselves. They do not use their conditions to manipulate, mistreat, or exploit others.

Self-care is taking the power that God has given you to make your-self the best you, you can be. This glorifies God, builds your own confidence, and sends a message to others that you have self-worth, that you are valuable. You really are valuable! Protect yourself, respect yourself, and stand up for yourself. Another part of self-care is assertiveness.

Assertiveness and love are partners. It is a high form of self-care. The assertive person has learned and understands how to be their own person firmly, confidently, and respectfully. They are not passive, not allowing others to walk all over them; and they are not aggressive, not trying to walk all over others. They are balanced, self-responsible people. Because we care for and value ourselves, we assert ourselves. We also care for and value others and allow them to be responsible for themselves too. This is a high form of love and why God gives us our own free will.

Assertive people practice getting what they want, learning, and meeting their own needs without harming others. They also allow people to take responsibility for their own needs. The assertive person will not feel guilty because someone else needs to mature in this area. As we grow more successful in assertiveness, we do not support irresponsibility and manipulation in others to control us. We are not selfish. We are practicing responsibility.

Assertive people do not take other people's consequences personally. Others are given the opportunity to learn, grow, and be responsible for themselves whether they want to or not. They are free to experience the results of their personal choices and learn from them. Loving ourselves and others this way is very liberating. While being assertive does not imply heartlessness to others' misfortunes, it draws a serious line of response for them. Manipulators like to control, blame-shift, and bully their life responsibilities onto others. They also systematically tear down and abuse those who succumb to their manipulations. The assertive person will not allow this because they care for themselves. They understand their personal boundaries and keep them in place to protect themselves. They understand where they stop and where others begin. Personal assertion is a boundary. Assertion does not facilitate enabling behaviors.

Love has boundaries.

> Above all else, *guard your heart*, for it is the wellspring of life. (Proverbs 4:23 NIV; emphasis added)

Love others with boundaries. Do not let anyone waltz in and out of your life whenever they want to, even if they are related to you. Jesus stayed on schedule with his Father's work, and His mother and siblings had to wait. (Read Luke 8:19–21.) Jesus wasn't ignoring them. He would not be sidetracked from His responsibilities, even by immediate family. He pointed out that those who loved God are His family. They wanted to interrupt His work for no particular reason.

It could have been just to rub shoulders with Him while He was popular. We are also cautioned in Scripture to be careful in friendships (Proverbs 12:26). We can be friendly and exercise discretion with close ties. Loving with boundaries protects you and others by reducing dysfunctional or inappropriate interactions, attachments, expectations, exploitation, and personal harm. Some people come with cartloads of heavy baggage they want others to carry for them or participate in like a soap opera. Targets of toxic people in relationships usually have damages resulting from a lack of assertion and boundaries in themselves. They are groomed to be overly responsible for others, usually beginning at very young ages, and it reappears in adulthood as codependency and enablement.

Guarding your heart is proactive behavior. Understand as much as you can about yourself and take measures to improve those areas in need of work.

When communicating with and loving others, practice some healthy boundaries:

1. *Trust is earned, not given.*
2. *Trust your gut.* Intuition is a gift from God to safeguard us.

3. *Take your time.* Get to know people. Everyone is on their best behavior and charming at the beginning. Pray, wait, and see what develops.

4. *Do not touch!* People hungry for physical connection, especially sensual physical connection, hang themselves in the spider's web! *Touch bonds you to the web, not the spider!* You have never seen a spider stuck in its own web. Resist this temptation for your own well-being!

5. *Do not disturb.* Have limitations of contact or responses to others; otherwise, you will be expected to provide instant access always; and this becomes a huge nuisance, especially during work, church, bedtime, or personal time. Texts, emails, calls, and social media activity will consume you if you let it! Do not let this happen!

> The apostles gathered around Jesus and reported to him all they had done and taught. Then, because so many people were coming and going that they did not even have a chance to eat, he said to them, "Come with me by yourselves to a quiet place and get some rest." (Mark 6: 30–31 NIV)

6. *Be careful not to jump into others' situations too quickly.* You can be swept away from your own responsibilities in others' drama. Pause, pray, and respond with wisdom.

7. *Do not bond over junk and baggage or let others dump on you.* Pray and respond with wisdom.

8. *Do not share personal information too quickly about yourself or those close to you.* Predators are experts at weaponizing the information you give them.

9. *Finally, when loving yourself and others, guard whom you allow into your personal space.* Jesus loved everyone, but He did not let everyone into His closest circle or personal space. Even among His disciples, He only let Peter, James, and John come with him into the Garden of Gethsemane

to pray during His most difficult period prior to His cruci-fixion. (Read Luke 22:39–46.)

Love does not require us to completely expose ourselves to everyone we care for. Some of those we care for do not need to be too close to us for a variety of reasons.

Toxic people and NPS individuals are like mold. They wait for the right conditions to spread themselves all over everything in your life until that place is a health hazard or condemned. The NPS indi-vidual wants to know everything about you—your family, your job, your friends, *everything!* They enjoy poaching relationships—that is, moving in to divide and conquer other people's close relationships or marriages. They make themselves available for illicit interactions because this makes them feel attractive and powerful. They mirror your best qualities to make your loved ones believe they are trust-worthy. They seduce and latch on to anyone they can use to hurt you. They want to snatch up opportunities to feed their sick need for NPS supply, which leaves a path of destruction. Be careful! *Love is not reckless.*

Harnessing the power of love God's way is a healing balm. It is powerful, hopeful, protective, beautiful, life-giving and produces peace, joy, and patience. God's love gives our hearts a much-needed rest because life can be exhausting. *He is here, filling us with His love and power.*

CHAPTER 7

The Power of a Sound (Disciplined) Mind

THE LAST BUILT-IN app is a sound mind. God wants our minds to be capable, healthy, righteous, peaceful, joyful, and full of faith and trust in Him. He also wants us to have life skills, focus, wisdom, understanding, hope, and rest. *We have been given a sound mind!*

Wex Definitions Team for Cornwall Law School stated that a sound mind and memory refer to a persons' state of being at the time of making their will. *A sound mind and memory means the person has sufficient mental capacity to understand their actions* (law.cornell.edu July 7, 2022). Wex stated that if someone contests a will, the court will examine whether the person understood what possessions they owned, whether the person understood the relationship between them and the people receiving their possessions, and whether the person understood the meaning and effect of the will (Wex 2021). This is powerful legal information.

God is more powerful in His legislation.

God wants us to understand what He has given to us and the relationship it has with our connection to Him and our lives. God gives us a sound mind so that we are capable to not only understand and know His will and choose our actions but also be able to choose blessings.

A sound mind is built in support. Although God gives this to us, it is our responsibility to discipline our minds. A sound mind is a disciplined mind. We must decide what to allow into our minds and what to let go. We must choose to think about things that are blessed, excellent, encouraging, strengthening, and peaceful. Disciplined mental behavior is always learning, new skills, better paths in life, and discretion. It also practices rejecting that which God disapproves.

I believe three pillars support our sound minds: courage, purpose, and contentment. We must plant and cultivate these pillars for support.

Planting means that the process begins with a seed and then must be cared for and cultivated to get the full fruit of the attribute. Remember, seeds are tiny but powerful. A seed is a decision or a concept planted in one's mind that can yield awesome results.

Courage is "will do despite fear." Fear affects us like a stun gun at times. It can immobilize a person. Imagine lying fully awake and unable to do anything, unable to move a muscle. Terrible! God consistently told everyone He worked miraculously through and for not to fear or be discouraged! This was the command before battles, during pilgrimages, during natural disasters, in the face of threats, before promotions to great wealth and affluence, and in the struggles of poverty. He commanded courage before miraculous deliverance from enemies and bondage. *Living freely requires courage!*

When the *Lord* tells us not to fear, He also tells us not to be discouraged, and then God gives us one awesome reason: *because He is with us!*

> So do not fear, for I am with you; be not dismayed, for I am your God. I will strengthen you and help you; I will uphold you with My righteous right hand. (Isaiah 41:10 NIV)

The seed of courage is the decision to take courage. When we plant and cultivate that, can-do power is activated. We can proceed with wisdom in courage and begin rejecting old useless mental habits that keep us from moving forward. It takes courage to take action to help yourself with God's help.

It also takes courage to stand still. We often associate courage with action, but standing still is an action that requires courage! It is the action of patience and restraint. Sometimes God tells us to stand still and see the salvation of the *Lord*! God is helping us every day!

Taking courage begins in your mind because you have to make up your mind to do or not do something and also to let go of something.

People suffering in toxic relationships are full of turmoil and fear because of their own personal issues that lock them in. Remember, our condition sometimes coordinates with the NPS individual. A deep fear of worthlessness, loneliness, boredom, helplessness, or disobedience to God and being discarded grips the mind. Fearing the loss of an idealized relationship is a heavy burden. We must let go of that toxic mindset. It poisons our reasoning and chokes out hope.

A new, excellent idea is necessary, one of a healthy, better life. A courageous mind must face these fears to eradicate them! Courage helps us detach from erroneous thinking, negative hopeless feelings, gloom, and toxic relationships.

God is holding our hands and supporting us in our journey to recovery and complete wellness.

The pleasure you experience from courage will have a wonderful effect on you. It rewires our brains to crave more courage. We begin to reap what we have sown—a crop of courage! As we live courageously, our self-esteem rises and provides a lift that shifts us from hopeless to powerful visionaries. Our lives become full of hope and possibilities because we are willing to do what we must to get where we want. Courage will have a snowball effect of benefits if we choose it.

The NPS individual feels the power shift and begins tactics to pull you back into a fearful position. It is very important for them to keep you obsessed about what they are doing. Expect some drama as they try to refocus your attention back onto them!

They know that if you stop watching and worrying about them, you will eventually let go and take care of yourself. The fear of losing control of the charade you once hoped was love is all that's left for them to try to manipulate. They may give you a short love flood (to romance you back under their influence), threaten your value by triangulating you with someone else that's "better," or employ the good, old-fashioned silent treatment. All this is to distract you from courageously focusing on life apart from their antics. Resist them, take courage, and trust God. Keep your focus on your goals for a better life.

Do not fear! The Lord is with you! You are getting better and stronger every day! *Congratulations!*

Stay focused. Look forward with awareness of your surroundings. No one can drive safely when only looking behind instead of forward. Know where you are going or where you hope to go, and you will get to your destination!

One of the reasons people in NPS/toxic relationships have difficulty leaving them is incorrect focus. Targets can be captivated by the NPS individual's every move. Thinking about, complaining about, talking about, and scavenging for more wrongdoing is the horrendous cycle of fear and dread of losing the relationship with your toxic loved one. This produces crazy hypervigilance. Imagine that! Fearing losing the relationship that makes your life a living hell. *Crazy*, right? The NPS individual wants to discard you when they are finished with you and not before! They do not want you to detach and leave on your own. If the NPS individual is immediate family, a relative, your boss, or some durable acquaintance, you must focus on strong boundaries. Anyone that has NPS or is toxic that you can let go of, let them go!

> But if the husband or wife who isn't a believer insists on leaving, let them go. In such cases the believing husband or wife is no longer bound to the other, for God has called you to live in peace. (1 Corinthians 7:15 NLT; obtained by biblegateway.com on August 2, 2022)

If this is true for married people, it is a useful rule for family and friends as well. Letting go does not mean that you do not love them.

It means that you stop engaging in toxic behavior and interactions with them. You are not trying to threaten, control, or change them. They just cannot remain active in your life, poisoning you. Pray for them, wish them well, release them and their antics to God, and move forward. Focus on better things ahead. Focus on your purpose for life or at least finding your purpose.

Purpose is the second pillar of a sound mind (i.e., a disciplined mind). Purpose is your whats and whys in life, your reasons for your actions. Purpose will help you choose how to focus your energy and attention in life. When you know what you want to do and why, you make choices to support it. You may encounter some distractions, some challenges, and some obstacles, and opposition may come. But purpose keeps you going. Purpose is deeper than a goal because it is essential to your life. Purpose is not just your profession or ministry; it is your motivation to activate the courage productively to live the abundant life God wants you to experience.

You must because! Visualize your life the way you want it to be. Do you want to be productive, strong, happy, self-sufficient, independent, and thriving? Do you want to experience real love and joy? Do you want confidence, peace, and success? Fine! You alone have to go after these for yourself.

In Scripture, regarding Israel and the Promised Land, God told them where it was and incrementally walked them through the process and each battle to go in and possess the land. He will do the same for us.

Purpose can be multifaceted but not double-minded. For example, we need deliverance from toxic relationships and also learn how to avoid bondage in them all together yet still have the courage to explore good relationships. This is a multifaceted purpose. It has multiple skill-set requirements and practices to support its success. The crucial activity we are working on as a whole is a healthy, caring relationship with ourselves and others.

Purpose supports goals. If you want to remain in a toxic intimate relationship and get out at the same time, you will fail because that is being double-minded. A single-minded (focused) aspiration is to do for yourself what you wish someone else would do for you. Now you're taking responsibility for yourself and have a purpose.

Disregard opposing ideas in favor of courage and purpose. If you have ever gardened or seen a garden, you know what flowers, vegetables, or desirable plants look like. When I was gardening, I found it interesting that many plants have weeds that look similar to them during their growth stages. The weed is revealed at harvest time when it does not produce the flower, fruit, or vegetable.

I planted black-eyed Susans one year, and they did not produce flowers. I left them in the ground, and the second year, they bloomed. The plants that looked almost identical to the black-eyed Susans had a slight and almost unnoticeable difference in leaf structure. The following season, I looked for plants with the different leaf formation and pulled them out early before they could choke out the flowers I wanted.

Weeds use up the water, fertilizer, space, and sun that desirable plants need. As we are discovering or active in our purpose, false success may pop up along the way. That's normal. We will learn to recognize and discard weeds in our lives. We will also learn not to live in fear, rejecting gardening because weeds exist.

We will learn to recognize weeds as early as possible and keep on growing. This lesson can be applied to toxic relationships and our own behavior. Managing our purpose and continuing to grow will also need the third pillar of a sound mind: contentment.

Contentment is the third pillar of support for a sound mind; it is the power to be satisfied. No matter what anyone has in life or who they are with, if one is not content, satisfied, or happy with what they have, strife is present. And discontentment is a troublemaker!

> What is causing the quarrels and fights among you? Don't they come from the evil desires at war within you? You want what you don't have, so you scheme and kill to get it. You are jealous of what others have, but you can't get it, so you fight and war to take it away from them. Yet you don't have what you want because you don't ask

God for it. And even when you ask, you don't get it because your motives are all wrong- you want only what will give you pleasure. (James 4:1–3 NLT)

In my opinion, lack of contentment is the black hole of antisocial disorders. People who do not know how to experience satisfaction in life become self-destructive, striving for contentment the wrong way. People can also be destructive because they hate their lack of contentment, so they want to destroy what they believe makes others happy. This is a dangerous state to remain in. It's aggravating! Learn to be content!

The easiest targets for predators are the weak, the injured, the lonely, and the discontent.

Contentment is a state, and so is discontentment. Escape from the NPS web is not possible without contentment because discontentment is the breeding environment for desperation and neediness. Discontentment makes targets needy for fulfillment. Discontent in NPS personalities is a bottomless pit because it never ends for them. Remember how both conditions have coordinating dance moves? You're stuck in a web, trying to find fulfillment in an illusion. They spin a web to catch a target to drain them and temporarily fill their emptiness.

The target may learn contentment, but the NPS individual always needs supply. It runs right through them no matter how excellent it is. They despise their source during and after consumption and are perpetually discontent and empty.

We must learn to be content even while working through difficulties; otherwise, we set ourselves up for permanent unhappiness. God is not anti-pleasure. He is antidestruction. He does not want people destroying themselves or others because they do not practice contentment.

Many things feed people's discontentment and produce personality and behavior disorders. God is pleased to give us what we want when we want the right things for appropriate reasons. He also wants us to decide to be satisfied on every level of life, or we will never experience joy.

We should grow as individuals, and part of personal development is accepting our blessings and not envying others' blessings. Comparing ourselves to others, covetousness, envy, and conceit are some of the reasons people are not satisfied.

People may also actually lack legitimate needs in their life, and improvements are in order. *The key is the ability to experience satisfaction in oneself as we are growing and learning in our way, not despising ourselves or others' accomplishments or possessions.*

Develop contentment by practicing gratitude. When we are thankful, we find good things to focus on, even in hardship. Thankfulness makes us appreciate God, ourselves, others, and whatever we do have, and this makes us less needy. We also can decide to be content no matter what. For example, your current situation is painful but also an awesome lesson equipping you for a better future. Thank God for the lessons you are learning.

Content people are not probing the world for people to give them joy in life. They take responsibility for themselves and desire balanced relationships. They also know that courage, purpose, and contentment support them and that they and God produce these qualities within themselves.

Armed with validation, awareness, and self-empowerment, we are in an excellent position to extract ourselves from the NPS/toxic web. *We can escape the spider!*

We are changing and getting better, so our lives are changing for the better.

Be kind to yourself. This behavior, with practice, will become an automatic lifestyle. Spiders and weeds will remain in this world, but we will manage ourselves better, keep our gardens weeded, and be aware of the spiders.

God bless you as you learn to enjoy His unconditional love and help! He has given us a spirit of power, love, and a sound (disciplined) mind. With these gifts and God's help, we can say goodbye to our spider!

CHAPTER 8

The Effort of Extraction

ALL MOUNTAIN CLIMBERS decide to climb their mountain. Instead of worrying about the challenge, they enjoy conquering the challenge. Once they decide to scale the mountain, they consider how to prepare for what they may encounter on the way up. Climbers plan safety measures for going up and catching them in case they slip so that they do not fall all the way back down. The successful mountain climber plans the adventure accordingly and is well prepared. The tools and supplies are strong enough to support the climber and are relevant to the mountain. Some mountains are lush and full of life. Others are harsh and desolate with jagged rocks. The climber packs for each terrain! They also prepare their bodies and minds to accomplish the journey. We will do the same!

> I called on the LORD, who is worthy of praise and He saved me from my enemies. (Psalm 18:3 NLT)

> God arms me with strength, and He makes my way perfect. He makes me as surefooted as a deer, enabling me to stand on mountain heights. (Psalm 18:32–33 NLT)

Getting out of the web of a toxic relationship takes effort. Do not give up because it takes effort! God is going to help you. You are going to help yourself. Everything that you need will be available at the right time with God's help. Make up your mind, trust in the *Lord*, and get ready. *Merriam-Webster* defines *effort* as a conscious exertion of power.

Cambridge Dictionary defines *effort* as a physical or mental activity needed to achieve something or an attempt to do something.

Nothing great is accomplished without conscious exertion of power along with physical and mental activity.

Mentally let go and detach with love to begin moving forward. One of the mysteries of people involved in narcissistic-personality-syndrome (NPS) relationships is the difficulty with the initial decision and ability to let go! I heard someone ask how long it takes to let go of a hot pan handle. Yet targets hold the hot handle and burn at times. Holding on is a strange response to something so uncomfortable and damaging. The difficulty of detaching from a toxic loved one and letting go of trying to change things or hoping they will change must not deter you from moving forward yourself. You may love them, but you must be responsible and loving toward yourself. God only holds us responsible for our own behavior in life!

Letting go may be difficult even with everything necessary in place, and this is because this situation is not just a toxic relationship. It is an addiction.

Addiction is what sticks you in the web! People fear going cold turkey and avoid rehab because of the discomfort of not using. Mental and physical attachment has created a kind of sticky chemical dependency. I will explain this later.

Another difficulty is finding supporting people and resources. Many people try to talk to others who they believe can support or help them during this difficult period; but it is amazing how many counselors, psychiatrists, and clergy resort to cookie-cutter methods. The wrong help is not help. It can actually make things worse.

Pressure from feeling isolated makes it tempting to give up. Do not give up! Just remember why people cannot help: they just don't understand, and they have either been duped by the NPS individual or are closed-minded to things they haven't experienced.

Close family and friends are part of the audience wooed by the same spider. They are charmed! They think something is wrong with you for not wanting this "wonderful" person. Some people will even envy what they believe you have. The majority of readily available help is people struggling to survive and share their stories on YouTube, in blogs, or in books. Lack of relevant professional help is one consistent factor in many of these people's stories. Those experienced with NPS-/toxic-relationship terrain may be your best choice for support because they understand and have come through the jungle successfully. (Avoid sites and groups where people complain more than work at getting free.)

I will also repeat often that *God is with you*. He knows the deal and is present to help. God will open up the Red Sea for you when you decide to move forward, trusting Him and participating in your own miracle.

Remember after the Passover how God had Moses take the nation of Israel out of slavery from the Egyptians? They walked out loaded with resources and very shortly met the first impassable obstacle. Just as they realized they were blocked, Pharaoh decided to go after them and drag them back into slavery. God blocked Pharaoh's efforts and made an impossible passage *possible* for Israel! What's even more amazing is that what was a miraculous route of escape for Israel was the doom of the pursuing enemies of their freedom!

This story is an amazing demonstration of God's dedication to help those who trust in Him for deliverance from bondage. You can read about it in the Bible book Exodus.

Decide—the first step to any action is a decision. So make a choice and keep moving forward. Do not overthink your decision. You are not hating but loving when you chose to save your life. Do pray and ask God for wisdom and keep your eyes on the prize—your improved life. Toxic relationships are full of deception and manipulation, so it is difficult to make decisions at times. We are coerced into self-doubt often when our NPS partner denies what is in plain view, so we learn to doubt our judgment. So it is important to understand yourself and your reasons in an easy way.

Ask yourself questions—for example, "Why do I want to let go of this relationship?" Be honest with yourself and do not try to justify the mess.

Do not worry about the audience (those friends, relatives, and others closest to you). You will find yourself making a lot of progress (not including those under the NPS individual's charm) about any of the details regarding your decision to let go.

Decide to find a support system somewhere. By *support*, I mean someone, an organization, or a group, if you can, for encouragement. Keep this book handy for encouragement. You are making a powerful decision, choosing to remove yourself from toxic bondage. It is a covert form of abuse. You will need encouragement to stay motivated in your decisions and actions.

Act! Taking action means that your efforts support your goal, and you must continue to resist distractions. Brainstorm what you must do to free yourself. Understand the truth about why you hang on and resolve that. For example, if you are lonely, learn to make healthy connections. If you need financial support, reduce your expenses and learn to manage your finances or get a job if that's the issue. Remind yourself why you are making these decisions. This book is written to help you as much as possible and was intentionally formatted to be biblically supported.

I find that outside of withdrawal symptoms, the second-largest obstacle to extracting oneself from toxic relationships is the fear that God does not approve. We may believe that it is unloving or unforgiving to let go of toxic relationships, but it is not.

God approves of healthy relationships and tells us to let go of wicked people. There is more biblical support for keeping wicked people out of our lives than not. I believe that people confuse boundaries with unforgiveness. They are also confused about true forgiveness, and there is a whole chapter about that.

This book is largely focused on intimate NPS/toxic relationships but can be used for any dysfunctional relationship. You will notice that I repeat some things. I am not trying to be redundant. I want the message to be clear. We can be prone to hear and interpret life solely on what we are used to experiencing and miss important messages. Repeating information is helpful.

Here is an example: I went to a store with my receipt to return an item. The return clerk asked me if I had a receipt. I held it up and said yes. She went on and on about how she could not give me a refund without a receipt. Again I tried to give her my receipt. She finally took it and continued explaining that only with a receipt could a refund be approved. After multiple complaints about people without receipts, she looked unbelievingly at mine, now still in her hand, and with a disgruntled look on her face, gave me a refund. This person was so used to people harassing her for refunds without a receipt that she couldn't hear me or see my receipt until after multiple attempts. She was firmly in gear to deal with the same ol' hassle.

We might need to hear things more than once to get the message. It is okay as long as we get the right message. Four areas that affect our extraction from the web are biological, mental, emotional, and spiritual. We must understand and prepare to manage these.

CHAPTER 9

Biological Bondage

WHEN PEOPLE SAY that they have chemistry between them, they are correct. I am not a chemist, a doctor, a scientist, but believe me when I tell you that chemistry exists between people.

No one has to be a chemist to understand that we experience different feelings around different people for different reasons. Stress, happiness, anxiety, relaxation, hate, romance, love, security, defensiveness, fear, peace, and so on manifest in our bodies because emotions are mental and chemical. These emotions and thoughts affect our bodies, and our bodies are full of chemicals naturally. Folks understand from the effects of certain chemicals that they hate or enjoy certain people. Sweaty palms, blushing, cold sweats, nervous ticks, sexual excitement, racing hearts, flushed faces, and upset stomachs are some of the biological responses to chemistry between people.

Biological relates to the body. People like pleasure chemicals, and the more pleasure we derive from something, the more we tend to crave and engage in it. (This is why some people will do anything for likes on social media.)

Four chemicals in the brain that affect pleasure and happiness are the following:

1. *Dopamine.* It is the striving emotion chemical anticipating happiness.

2. *Oxytocin.* It is neurochemical for social connections and empathy.
3. *Serotonin.* It is our mood chemical, good mood also present 80 percent gut hunger.
4. *Endorphins.* It masks pain or discomfort and is responsible for our fight-or-flight response (technologyadvice.com).

The acronym for dopamine, oxytocin, serotonin, and endorphins is DOSE.

Gamified experiences produce DOSE and keep us coming back for more. These chemicals are very addictive. The dynamics of NPS/toxic relationships are very similar to gamification and mass-produce DOSE, locking people in gaming addiction. Which is why in the face of pain and devastation, people keep coming back for more. They are addicted, and they believe it's because of love. The strong draw is addiction!

Gamification is the application of typical elements of game playing (i.e., point scoring, competition with others, and rules of play) to other areas of activity, typically as an online marketing technique to encourage engagement with a product or service (Lexico, powered by Oxford, 2019).

Toxic relationships are full of games. Most NPS persons are not masterminding these behaviors; they are natural to them. It is how they attempt to meet their needs. These patterns of behavior ingrained in them are the result of how they are wired. They also notice what gets them the results they desire and repeat what works for them. Bringing this to their attention will not improve them or you. Being aware of this will help you protect yourself when you notice them one way or another.

Gazelles understand that lions like to eat them, so they graze with their attention on high alert in the presence of lions. By the way, wherever there are gazelles, there are lions. Another fact to remember is that when NPS persons are moving through their relationship stages, they experience the rush also! They feel the chemistry too! They are also addicted to chemistry!

During *idealization*, you feel the rush, and they feel the rush! During this phase, they believe you are perfect for them because of the rush! They are excited about extending your best attributes to themselves, and this is great energy (i.e., supply) for them. It makes them look and feel good. If you are a mess and they target you, it makes them look heroic because they are noble for loving a mess. It is all supply and chemistry for you both.

Tons of dopamine and oxytocin are flooding your brain. You are so excited! *But* while you are anticipating true love and connection, they are anticipating egocentric fulfillment and admiration from this event and the possible next supply! A strong bond is forming quickly (you to the web and they to their idea of you that benefits them). Both of you want to feel like this will last forever, but it will stop.

Next, *during the love flood,* the NPS individual wants to secure this new idea, and so do you. The romance begins with over-the-top wonderful behavior. It comes in like a wall. Like a tsunami! Now a rush of serotonin is roused. It feels so good! The bond is getting stronger, and the tidal wave of "love" is coming in. Think about how tsunamis affect the environment.

Tsunamis (tidal waves) are caused by underground earthquakes in the ocean, specifically earthquakes from shifting titanic plates. This is similar to how the relationship begins. You both are shifting, especially you! The NPS individual does not have normal emotions, just a never-ending need. They rush in like a tsunami heading inland from the ocean. The wall of water is pushing everything forward in its path or knocking structures down as it moves in. When it cannot go in any further, the tsunami retreats and moves back to the ocean, further damaging everything on its way out. It is dragging the wreckage and everything in the exit path back out when it goes.

This is how the NPS individual and the target experience what they think is love. They move in powerfully, sweeping you off of your feet. Later you find that you were just swept away and then trashed. In intimate relationships, sexual involvement cements the bond even more. The better the sex, the more bonded you become because that is incorporated into the addictive chemistry already sealing you in.

The tsunami retreat—that is, the love flood going out—is the devaluing-and-detaching chemistry. You are now about to experience the endorphin-mass-production phase of the relationship! Coming down off the high of all the pleasure chemicals to feeling threatened is sickening. You do not understand your health and mental problems at this point. They feel it too and go quickly into denial because they need to get back on the pleasure wave, and you are not new to them anymore no matter what you do. They are probing for new supply, and you are suffering. You are experiencing fight-or-flight chemistry no matter what they say to assure you of their love, and this is because you feel the disconnect in your gut and are going through withdrawal.

The withdrawal symptoms produce adrenaline rushes because your brain perceives the threat of the relationship ending, and it is terrible. Subconsciously you feel like your life is in danger because that's how intense this is.

Adrenaline is produced by our bodies to help with sudden threats and danger! NPS individuals feel threatened too, which is why they are so distracted. They feel supply dwindling for them. Nothing you do can help this! You want them lovingly close to make you feel better, and they want out. The NPS individual will keep you around to drain you until they are sure they have a new source. They want to get back to feeling high on adventure and love. They need a completely new idealization, and you are not it.

The *devaluing-and-detaching phase* can be short or long; it just depends on how fast either of you can get out. They want you intact until they are secure. Stress and chemical reactions leading to adrenaline overload begin to ruin your health. This is the most damaging phase because they will employ tactics to keep you still while they set up what they want elsewhere. You are desperate to communicate your feelings and want to restore intimacy. You can sense the insidious behaviors of them leaving and staying simultaneously. Your body senses the threat. Stress is abundant during this phase.

Endorphins help you go into denial because they help mask pain and unpleasant emotions. Adrenaline tells you to protect yourself quickly! You feel hyped up to save the relationship, and then something else develops. These two chemicals help develop a condition: cognitive dissonance!

Cognitive dissonance happens when two sets of data or information that contradict each other coexist. The associated chemicals—endorphins and adrenaline—also coexist in your body, and it is disturbing. You feel the danger of your relationship ending. You feel and see all the symptoms of the disconnect. They deny that anything is wrong and assure you that the relationship is secure. You notice very tiny incremental cracks in the things they say and do. You want to believe them and relax, but your intuition tells you that you are experiencing a lie. Cognitive dissonance will tempt you to choose the lie, what you wish was happening, because it is temporarily comforting.

It is evident that you are not getting what you want, but you are tempted to go into denial.

Now you have what I call a coin! A coin has a front (heads), and it also has a back (tails). Both sides are on the same coin! You can't have one without the other. Targets will now try to calm down the chemical chaos in their bodies and minds with cognitive dissonance. They pick a side of the coin, hoping the other side will go away. Regardless of whether you pick heads or tails, the side that you do not want is still present, and you are stressed out and getting sicker.

Stress is how your body responds to good or bad stimuli. Purchasing your first home is exciting, and it is stressful, although the situation is good. Losing a beloved pet is stressful because it is sad. Both situations produce stress. The mixed pleasure and danger chemicals of cognitive dissonance are destructive to your health and well-being.

CHAPTER 10

Chemical Reactions and You

$S_{AVING\ THE\ RELATIONSHIP}$ *is the goal of the target.* Using the relationship to the last drop until new supply is secured is the goal of the NPS individual. These opposing goals along with cognitive dissonance give way to another addictive element: gamification. I mentioned this earlier. This provides another kind of rush that keeps both people engaged in a ruined situation while providing DOSE. (Remember dopamine, oxytocin, serotonin, and endorphins?)

The target and the NPS individual are highly addicted to DOSE, and gamification keeps it going. Toxic relationships are full of games. The dramatic beginnings, conflicts, breakups, deceptions, hide-and-seek, adventure for wrongs and rights, and scoring are addictive. Competition with others not only includes the target but also the other/s the NPS individual pits against the target in triangulation (love triangles). These boost the NPS individual's ego and is supply for them. Exciting games are highly addictive, which is why they are in astounding demand in technology, casinos, sports, and (sadly) relationships.

Slot-machine syndrome, in relation to the NPS individual, is the thrilling activity of trying for a jackpot—true love! This produces DOSE! Slot-machine syndrome is when the NPS individual offers you a jackpot (an innuendo) of love, and that produces hope in you!

Hope gets you going! You begin inserting *your tokens* (i.e., whatever they imply or you believe that they want from you for the relationship to get back to happiness). As you are pouring your tokens into them (the slot machine) and pulling the lever (trying to please them), hoping to win a normal, healthy relationship, you will notice constant fake jackpots, small periods of niceness. You will also notice that for the real jackpot (love), you are always one cherry short!

Tokens, going broke, and more chemical reactions—it is expensive to play this game because tokens cost you your life! Tokens can be believing their lies; not asking questions; hiding your pain (that they tell you, you shouldn't be experiencing); keeping up fronts in public; tolerating infidelity; giving them access to your friends, family, children, or money; tolerating neglect or various abuses; and much more. The point is you can pour in a river of these tokens, and you will not win! You will crave the DOSE, but you must resist it and stop playing! Save your life by not inserting it into this losing game.

Adrenal fatigue is another biological effect of the NPS relationship. Adrenaline is a helpful chemical that God gave us to help us act fast to protect ourselves in the face of imminent danger. Our pulse quickens, our thoughts sharpen, our blood gets thicker in case of injury, and our bodies get ready to run or fight! It helps us defend ourselves!

Adrenal fatigue is a condition that develops when we are constantly feeling threatened or very stressful for long periods of time. Adrenaline was not designed to flow all day every day through our bodies. It is an on-demand chemical. Targets stay flooded with adrenaline because daily they feel the undercurrent of threats to their well-being in this highly toxic relationship. Hypervigilant behaviors and walking on eggshells exhaust our adrenal glands, which produce this chemical for our protection. Soon our bodies will not know how to regulate its supply for dispensing adrenaline because we need it all day long always! Because adrenaline is designed for massive action, it lies in our bodies until it is released through action. When we are sitting still because we are feeling depressed and exhausted and trying to figure out what we are going through, this chemical is building up in our bodies and not being used. The result of this buildup is nervous conditions, physical tics and sicknesses, panic attacks (when awake or asleep), burnout, and confusion.

Now it appears that we are, for lack of a better term, *nuts*! The NPS individual uses this against us. Being in a relationship with an NPS individual produces these results in targets, often even when a target chooses to let go. They may experience dramatic withdrawal symptoms similar to a drug addict going cold turkey. Some people think that these symptoms are fear or love holding them or drawing them back. I promise you that chemical addiction to DOSE is what's bonding you to this situation, not love. Understanding this is very important.

Preparing for freedom requires facing the truth. We must prayerfully and responsibly face the facts and trust God for help. He will get you through this and out of the web. I believe that it is best to pray for strength to go through withdrawal while you are still in the relationship if you can so that when you are out, all of the mess is left behind you. God will help you even with withdrawal symptoms if you have them.

> The righteous cry out, and the LORD hears them; He delivers them from all their troubles. The LORD is close to the brokenhearted and saves those who are crushed in spirit. (Psalm 34:17–18 NIV)

CHAPTER 11

Mental Transformation

V*ISUALIZE YOURSELF VICTORIOUS.* Visualize yourself not hurt when the NPS individual flaunts their new idea in front of you. Stop arguing with them. Stop trying to please them. Stop fearing that the new person they dote on is better than you. You are not in a competition. And stop trying to nullify accusations of you not caring for them. You care about them, but you are letting them and their antics *Go!*

Begin to do your best to take excellent care of yourself. Get rest and resist destructive coping behaviors such as using illicit drugs, exacting vengeance, overeating, turning to alcoholism, binge-shopping, or getting into rebound relationships. Exercise to release all of that adrenaline built up in your body. Above all, pray! Pray for strength and support from God. Read Scripture. Read the Serenity Prayer and other encouraging, uplifting things. Listen to inspirational, calming or happy, motivating music. Eat delicious, healthy food. Drink lots of fresh water. Work on or learn a relaxing hobby. Talk to your doctor if you need help with stress symptoms and any physical ailments. Mentally review, accept, and practice the lessons God is teaching you. Visualize yourself happy as an individual and surviving this successfully and wonderfully, because *you will!*

Therefore everyone who hears and practices
these words of mine and puts them into practice

is like a wise man who built his house on the
rock. The rain came down, the streams rose, and
the wind blew and beat against that house; yet it
did not fall, because it had its foundation on the
rock. (Matthew 7:24–25 NIV)

All the excellent advice and lessons in the world are useless
unless we hear and practice them. People's behavior must line up
with their goals for them to succeed.

The journey can be rewarding because improvement is always a
great adventure. It is exhilarating to take care of ourselves, especially
if we have always been dependent on others. We must commit to a
lifestyle of learning and personal development. Learning and practicing excellent behavior will transform and guard our lives. Lasting
excellent results are the result of building on a solid foundation.
When we build on rock, we can survive the storms.

Storms will always come, especially during storm season.
Building well is a safeguard against what will come. Wise people accept the reality of and prepare for storm seasons and stormy
weather. And also the storms of life.

As we move out of DOSE addiction and the web of NPS/toxic
bondage, a vacuum is being created in our lives that needs filling with
an excellent replacement.

We need a mental transformation! This is replacing the thinking
that gave place to the NPS situation, which could have consumed
us. Learn new things that are beneficial for your well-being and
think on these things. Learn new life skills. Learn from mistakes and
learn to keep on trying. Learn basic life skills if you lack them (e.g.,
personal care, self-control, self-motivation, and home management
[cleaning, paying bills, cooking, etc.]). Fill your mind up with good,
courageous, nourishing thoughts. Say good things to yourself and to
others. Repeat life-enriching affirmations to yourself. You can write
your own affirmations or write down any encouraging words that
you find.

Here are a few of my personal affirmations:

1. "God loves me and helps me every day, and I am so thankful!"
2. "I can do all things through Christ, who strengthens me."
3. "I am so loved!"
4. "My life is getting better every day!"
5. "I am very grateful for all that I have."
6. "I will love and care for myself better than I hoped someone else would."

> Don't copy the behaviors and customs of this world, but let God transform *you* into a new person by changing the way you think. Then you will learn to know God's will for you, which is good and pleasing and perfect. (Romans 12:2 NLT; emphasis added)

Our mind is the greatest tool needed for excellent living in this world. Our thoughts, emotions, and body are connected to support one another and also contribute to our true quality of life and survival. Understanding our own thoughts will help us understand the reasoning behind some of our needs and behaviors, which affect our decisions and outcomes.

We do not have to be experts to recognize and learn about our mental and emotional habits. We must be honest with ourselves to improve. Awareness of ourselves and our environment will aid us in life and in extracting ourselves from toxic relationships.

Remember the gazelles grazing and being aware? They do not despise being gazelles or complain about the lions. They did not go to college to learn that they are prey or that awareness and avoiding predators will save their lives. Gazelles know these things from experience and tragedy. They need to eat and drink water. They also know that lions have the same needs. Wherever they are, so are the lions! These are the primary facts that gazelles instinctively know that save their lives! *Oh*, and they run away—*fast*! When a lion pursues them, they run! This interaction between gazelles and lions is natural. Humans can learn from these animals. We are more complicated than them, but the simplicity of running from danger is helpful. This is why it is important to recognize toxic behaviors and listen to our intuition (our gut). If there is danger, *run!* Do not play games with your life.

> The prudent see danger and take refuge,
> but the simple keep going and pay the penalty.
> (Proverbs 27:12 NIV)

Know thyself and thy predator. Just being a gazelle automatically attracts lions. An NPS individual was not attracted to us for any other reason except that they are attempting to meet their own needs. We were attracted to them, also attempting to meet our needs. Their needs are complicated, and so are ours, and this is where the trouble begins. That irresistible paper-clip-sliding-toward-the-magnet response to toxic people is a signal that some internal changes are necessary. Everyone at some point can recall the faint warning in their gut—that little red flag or some warning that was ignored to engage this person. *Magnetism*, more than romance and sexual attraction, keeps this damaging dance going. Otherwise, it stops sooner than later.

Something within us was drawn to the toxic person and made us ignore the red flags, hoping to meet our needs. People also have a life history (a past) that contributes to who they are. Baggage from different significant periods of life develop our characters and attitudes and how we perceive life. This becomes a paradigm, and then we pick peculiar pastures (i.e., where we graze).

Our paradigm is simply our perspective, expectations, and responses to life because of what we have always experienced. Our paradigm may need to change. Transforming our thinking and how we see things will transform our experiences and lives! Part of the difficulty and frustration surrounding those affected by NPS and toxic people is the mountain of nonsense in both parties. We search frantically for the reasons that they do the things that they do and forget to dig deep within about why we do what we do. Why do we sit still and participate in all this bull crappery? If we get our reasoning together, we can kiss the spider goodbye because we will work on and resolve our issues that make us ignore the red flags. Not having red flags is like our cars missing brake lights. It's dangerous. Fix the brake lights!

The easiest way to get to the bottom of this toxic bond and detach is to ask yourself some questions and give yourself honest answers. What did the NPS individual do to disappoint or hurt you? Some of these areas will define the needs you expected them to meet in your life. Some will be legitimate expectations, and others will not be. For example, if they constantly make you feel bad about yourself, you may have been depending on them for self-worth. Our self-worth is not other's responsibility. Although put-downs are hurtful, they are not to be taken personally. Identify put-downs as emotionally abusive behavior. The solution to this is to learn to care for and value yourself. Practice throwing out the mental trash, just like discarding the poo we pick up when walking our dogs.

Begin doing what you need to for yourself. Learn also to disregard toxic criticism and manipulation as a lifestyle and keep moving forward. They need you to continue believing that your value lies in them, but it doesn't! The more secure you become in yourself, the more they will try to wear you down. Ignore this and continue building yourself up because you can!

Another example is if they never contribute to shared expenses, like utilities, and blame you for all the unpaid bills. You may need to learn to create boundaries. Understand that more drama will follow because they hate boundaries. Pay what you agreed on and decide how to survive if they still do not do their part. Just do not pick up what you are not responsible for. This is enabling.

If you live together, you may have to experience living without certain things to keep from enabling them to be irresponsible. If they do not live with you, you may have to learn to ignore blame for their lack. If kids are involved, toxic people do not mind neglecting children to hurt you. This manipulation is to put you back in the place they want you in—where you enable them and carry the entire load.

Find a good advisor to help advocate for the children, but do not give in.

NPS individuals have no problem playing dirty, even when others are hurt. Your issue may be lack of boundaries, codependency, or a need to learn and develop assertive skills. Address these!

One more example is if the NPS individual is two-faced or unfaithful. People in intimate relationships usually expect faithfulness from each other. Do not ignore the facts. Do not argue. This is tricky because this behavior usually involves high levels of deception, manipulation, and delusion.

Decide what you need to do, prayerfully uninhibited by rhetoric. By this I mean deciding if the relationship is worth saving for honest reasons regardless of what others think or say. Religious misconceptions about love and forgiveness can make you feel guilty for letting go of abuse and chronic unfaithfulness. Deeply ingrained consistently dishonest and unfaithful behavior is usually ongoing because these patterns are a lifestyle for the perpetrator. Some believers have horrible default behavior. Believing in Jesus Christ as your Savior will not make you change automatically into a wonderful person. A renewed mind takes time, repentance, and effort. Some people are not there yet. Scripture states that the foolish person is like a dog that will return to its vomit. In other words, they will return to their wicked behavior.

> As a dog returns to its vomit, so a fool
> returns to his folly. (Proverbs 26:11 TLB)

Practice mindful self-improvement. If you know that certain emotions trigger neediness in you, avoid trying to distract yourself from yourself. Face your issues and deal with them. Understand your triggers and how you feel about what is happening so that you can manage yourself better. It is amazing how after you do this for a while, you will not entertain ruining yourself by trying to extract out of others what you can do for yourself. Life changes for you. Now it's more rewarding to do without than settle for anything.

Do not waste time complaining and revealing all your plans on social media for attention, validation, and companionship. Develop time with God and yourself. Tell God about all your concerns and issues and ask for comfort, direction, and help. He will help you. Instead of anxiously focusing on your NPS partner, focus on yourself and how to improve your life. Refuse to settle for delusions; the fruit on a tree is what it is! Accept the truth about you and your situation. Resist diving into denial because you want someone else to change. Change yourself and learn to enjoy your life. You do have a life, and it is valuable to God and you.

CHAPTER 12

Emotion Motions

OUR EMOTIONS CHANGE *with our mental activity, behavior, and situations.* Extracting ourselves from toxic bonds will require us to analyze and detach from erroneous ideas, certain behaviors and activities, and false hope. This upsets some people because they believe it is wrong to let go of or give up on relationships—even toxic relationships!

Giving up or letting go of wrong is right! Give up wrong thoughts, wrong expectations, and wrong responses. Give up abuse, enablement, and unloving entrapment. Give up wrong to make room for what is right! And train your emotions to follow your decisions! *Britannica* defines *emotion* as a complex experience of consciousness, bodily sensation, and behavior that reflects the personal significance of a thing, an event, or a state of affairs (britannica.com).

Because emotions affect our decisions, they need management and discipline if we are to live happy and productive lives. Because emotions are closely tied to our senses, they have a powerful effect on our health, well-being, and decisions. It should be our aim to understand our emotions and learn how to manage them. By *understanding*, I mean knowing our whys and thinking about the possible outcomes of our decisions before allowing emotions to drive and rule us. We need to think about why we do what we do.

When we live only by our emotions, we are extremely vulnerable to manipulation. I like the way Ebenezer Scrooge put it in the classic story *A Christmas Carol*, by Charles Dickens (1843). Scrooge was haunted by Marley, his old business partner who died seven years before that Christmas. Marley's ghost asked Scrooge why he didn't believe in him although they were having a conversation.

> "Why do you doubt your senses?" asked Marley.
> "Because" said Scrooge, "a little thing affects them." (goodreads.com, July 15, 2022)

Emotions and senses are partners, and both must be guarded and managed. Advertising companies understand the power of people's emotions. To make an enormous impact in as little time as possible, marketers pour massive amounts of communication into tiny bits of time. They use imagery, music, behaviors, moods, actors, a product, and the script that pushes it all indelibly into the audience's mind. Super Bowl commercials are probably the most expensive and powerful advertisements of the year because they are very effective! Our hearts (i.e., our emotion, character, and behavior center) must be guarded!

> Above all else, *guard your heart,* for it is the wellspring of life. Let your eyes look straight ahead, fix your gaze directly before you. Make level paths for your feet and take only ways that are firm. Do not swerve to the right or left; keep your foot from evil. (Proverbs 4:23, 4:25–27 NIV; emphasis added)

How difficult it is to detach depends on what and how someone is attached. Our emotions/senses helped us buy into something that we now regret. Now we must get out of this transaction to reduce our losses.

Marketing refers to activities a company undertakes to promote the buying or selling of a product or service (investopedia.com). Marketing goals require them to meet the needs of the company and their stakeholders. That means they want to profit from their business. Companies want to get the attention of everyone that can potentially contribute to their profits. First, they reach out to the crowd that most likely will buy. Next are those closest to that crowd because of popularity. Finally, they reach out to those who they must convince to buy in, who have the greatest future market value. The NPS/toxic people do the same!

When they are selling, their objective (not yours) drives them. It doesn't matter if you hate pizza-flavored breakfast cereal. When they finish their high-powered systematic presentations, you'll think about or actually try it, as disgusting as it sounds. That is unless you stand your ground. Advertising reaches out to all minds and decides the best time to communicate their messages to accomplish their goals. Mindful guarding and prayer are proactive steps against such tactics.

You may wonder, What does this have to do with us? *We are the target market! The NPS people are the marketers!* Our state of mind and the NPS individual created a relationship/life transaction that has collateral damages. We must let go of what is wrong that will never be right to protect ourselves and those closest to us. We also must not continue buying. Remember, the audience (those closest to us) is under the influence of our toxic situation. Everyone watching sees and hears the commercials. Some are buying. Some are considering buying, or some have already bought.

The target market and sales tactics are relevant. Toxic people need targets to trust them. They purposefully manipulate others through various tactics. Whatever gets their needs met becomes a pattern for them. One of the ways they appeal to our trust is through a tactic called mirroring. Mirroring is them copying your values and pretending to be just like you.

Most people give others a portion of trust initially in the relationship as a baseline courtesy. We hope that others are as decent as we believe we are or more. We are doing this to, hopefully, begin a good relationship. This is true not only for intimate relationships but also community agencies as well as businesses, banks, mechanics, medical providers, friends, and churches, among others. People want to build on what they believe they can trust. Most people trust themselves, so who else is better for the NPS individual to replicate when building faux trust than the target!

They pay attention to us intently; absorb our preferences, values, interests, dislikes, religion, and so forth; and then reflect them back to us. "What a coincidence! You like that too! We have so much in common!" We let our defenses rest because what we are really doing is bonding with a reflection of ourselves. And they are just as bonded to us as the mirror that we look at to see a reflection of ourselves. On the cool, hard glass is just a reflection. Mirroring also helps them enjoy a false extension of themselves from you. They temporarily believe their own illusion, and that delusion ends soon. When it ends for them, they despise you. Mirrors are easily broken.

Some manipulators use the fear of abandonment to secure a bond with the target. Capturing a person's attention and communication in what seems like positive interest and then suddenly cutting off communication, only to pick it up again, is an NPS/toxic method of control. This activates dependence and neediness in the person who suffers from the fear of abandonment.

Future faking is another tactic. It encourages targets to believe that a commitment is pending. Innuendos of undying love and attraction sprinkled with contempt for anyone "jealous" of your relationship is not uncommon. Sometimes the NPS individual uses this tactic to get themselves into your closer circles. They shower you with affection and praise to impress the audience. Mudslinging will begin with this same group if you begin to or actually detach. Now a well-groomed collection of targets is ready to replace you.

Keep your keys to yourself. I do not know every tactic a toxic person has in their toolbox, but I do know this: it is critical that you practice mindful awareness of yourself and the communications you engage in, especially those that may become close to you. Keep your buttons, remotes, keys, behavior, and resources under your own control. Pay attention and pray for protection. I heard someone say once, "No one can drive you crazy unless you give them the keys" (unknown).

Detach yourself accordingly. Our thoughts and emotions got us into this mess and we will think and feel better to get ourselves out.

Remember that detaching does not mean that you hate or do not forgive the NPS/toxic persons. It is protective behavior, disengaging from toxic bonding.

> O righteous God, who searches minds and hearts, bring to an end the violence of the wicked and make the righteous secure. My shield is God Most High, who saves the upright in heart. God is a Righteous Judge, a God who expresses his wrath every day. (Psalm 7:9–11 NIV)

CHAPTER 13

Deconstruct and Detach

*Guard my life and rescue me; let me not be
put to shame, for I take refuge in You.*
—Psalm 25:20 NIV

DETACHMENT IS EXHAUSTING. It involves letting go of and being apart from things, ideas, and people we are deeply connected to. When we are attached, we need help getting out or letting go. I like this psalm because it is a good prayer for protection, rescue, reputation, and continued support. It is short, sweet, and powerful. Unhealthy attachments ruin many people's lives, yet it is still difficult to let go. God will help us do what we must do. Pray this psalm to encourage yourself.

Deconstruct and salvage—take everything apart carefully and enjoy the benefits of salvaging. Salvaging involves rescuing and retrieving valuables from the ruins. When we analyze our situation, there are takeaways that are very valuable to our lives. Do not trash the valuables of a demolition. There are many recyclables and upcyclables in the ruins. We can move on and be better, wiser, stronger, and full of benefits from the school of hard knocks. Demolition does not include trashing the toxic person. We pray for them, turn them over to God, and wish them well while detaching from the toxic relationship.

We can ask ourselves some very important questions. Here are some examples:

> Q1. What can I use from this event to improve my future?
> A1. Never ignore my gut and practice mindful self-care.
> Q2. How can I avoid repeating the same situation?
> A2. I can recognize my patterns of behavior when trying to meet my own needs, practice better choices, and take responsibility for myself. Live aware and run away from the lions.
> Q3. What addictive elements did I ignore that kept me stuck, and what does that mean?
> A3. Idealization and dramatic activities are addictive. I will improve my self-image, be responsible for the adventures in my life, and also resist codependent behavior.

There are many things to be thankful for even though it has been difficult. Ask God to help you with your takeaways. Do not waste energy complaining and grumbling. Salvage whatever you can to move forward and build better relationships in the future, beginning with knowing yourself better.

It is very important to decide to stop wasting life. I lived in a mobile home and had to move to another state. I was considering demolishing my small home because I couldn't afford to pay the lot rent for it and also the cost of living in another state. The only thing I could afford when relocating was a small fixer-upper. To avoid financial problems, I had to consider the cost of continuing to wait for my place to sell compared to the value of deconstructing and removing it from someone else's land. Mobile homes belong to the homeowner but are set up on parcels called lots in mobile-home communities belonging to a landowner. I knew that if I could sell my little home and make the new place livable, I would have a chance to do better financially. My new place suited all my needs, and I got a better-paying job in an area where it was convenient to live. And the cost of living was more manageable.

I decided on a stop-loss date—that is, the time I would cease investing in something that was not bringing me any returns or value. When I reached my stop-loss date, my only concern was letting go of the liability responsibly. It would cost me less to tear down and remove my mobile home than pay for an empty building to occupy someone else's land for another year.

I made a list of all the materials I could reuse in the place before demolition. This added to the value of my decision because the appliances, flooring, cabinets, etc. were in excellent condition and could be used to improve my new place. I thank God that it sold the month before my demolition date, and I used some of that money to accomplish good things in my new location. If I had deconstructed the home, I would have had many reusable items. My little story is applicable in any situation where we must let go.

The cost of holding on with no benefits is expensive and hinders us from moving forward.

Relevant detachment means the things I would have deconstructed required different detachment methods to remove and reuse them. Ceiling fans, cabinets, flooring, and other fixtures are nailed, glued, wired, screwed, and bolted into place. The best way to detach them was to use a detachment method compatible with how they were attached. Unscrewing, unwiring, pulling out nails, welding apart, cutting apart, digging up, and cracking out fixtures are hard work. We can deconstruct our toxic bond and take out the valuable lessons we have learned to help us live a better life.

For example, if we bonded over junk (i.e., problems and issues), detaching will require letting people handle their junk while we handle our own. Often, bonding over junk is usually codependent behavior. One person is fixing the other (usually an irresponsible person) in an attempt to repair themselves and gain relationship security. It is not the same as a support group, where individuals take responsibility for themselves but are working in a group setting. Our lives are improving, and awareness of what hooks us will help keep us free.

If the pain of detaching is too much and we give up trying, things can get even worse! Millions of people have a fear of going to the dentist. Those who practice the best dental hygiene can still get a cavity, and if it is not treated immediately, it will decompose into an abscess. The tooth now needs a root canal instead of a filling. If we dull the pain and ignore that treatment, it can continue to decay until an extraction is necessary. If we ignore that long enough, the decay can spread and become more infected and painful, requiring surgical extraction and cosmetic prosthetics.

The fear of the entire experience promotes avoidant behavior, and the condition gets worse. One day something begins to happen. The painkiller is not effective because of the infection. Now we need antibiotics. When the pain is so bad that it supersedes the fear of the dentist, then we face that fear and apply treatment to get rid of the cause of the unbearable infection and pain! How bad it needs to be before a decision is made is different for everyone in toxic relationships. It is my opinion that prevention is the best policy.

Pray and brainstorm for solutions. Seek help outside your audience to receive unbiased, untainted advice, preferably from those who understand your conflict. Do not threaten the NPS individual with the decision to help yourself. Just do it. There are people who have come through this successfully and can share advice and empathetic communication. That is the purpose of this book.

Finally, ask yourself, "What have I lost because of holding on to this relationship?" How much more are you willing to lose? Remember, we are not hating or not forgiving others. We are choosing to let go of a toxic relationship with a toxic person. Our relatives, siblings, employers, and other durable relationships may be toxic. We can love them and not include them intimately in our lives. Letting them go means cutting off the part of being with them that poisons us!

CHAPTER 14

Improving Our Spirits

*To you, O LORD, I lift up my soul; in You I trust,
O my God. Do not let me be put to shame, nor let
my enemies triumph over me. No one whose hope
is in You will ever be put to shame, but they will be
put to shame who are treacherous without excuse.
Show me your ways, O LORD, teach me your paths;
guide me in your truth and teach me, for you are
God my Savior, and my hope is in you all day long.*
—Psalm 25:1–5 NIV

IT HAS BEEN a long road, trying to find our way out of the web of toxic relationships. Some people give up hope because NPS (narcissistic personality syndrome) relationships are difficult and extremely unyielding. The struggle to understand if it is wrong or right to want out and how to get out wears people down. It is mentally, emotionally, and physically taxing! **The spiritual factor is the final but not least-important factor involved in escape and recovery.** Our spirit is the true self, the unseen part of our existence. Our spirit is the part of us that communicates with God. Our spirit is the life God breathed into us and makes us a living being.

> And the LORD God formed man of the dust
> of the ground, and breathed into his nostrils the
> breath of life; and man became a living soul.
> (Genesis 2:7 KJV)

The power to change our lives truly lies within our spirits. For it is in our spirit that we choose life!

> I call heaven and earth as witnesses today
> against you, that I have set before you life and
> death, blessings and curses. Now choose life,
> that both you and your descendants may live.
> (Deuteronomy 30:19 NKJV)

Spirit is life. It is also our attitude toward life. Think of team spirit, the way a person is excited about and supportive of a team. We need to protect our lives and learn to choose what supports and blesses our lives according to God's will.

Oxford Languages defines *spirit* as the nonphysical part of a person that is the seat of emotions and character of the soul (oxford-languages.com).

Merriam-Webster defines *spirit* as an animating or vital principle held to give life to physical organisms.

Our spirit is a powerful creative force that God Himself put into us. It not only gives us physical life but also helps us use our will to develop and express our divine purpose for existence. We are gifted to contribute to creation with the privilege of free will. We can choose to protect and enrich our environment or destroy and waste our environment. Everyone has something to contribute. We must first partake of this gift from God before we can share it with others. Just think. Someone had to create ice cream. I just contributed humor.

Just existing is not good enough. Jesus said that He came so that we might have life (i.e., exist) and life to the full (i.e., a fulfilling, abundant existence).

> The thief comes only to steal and kill and
> destroy; I have come that they may have life, and
> have it to the full. (John 10:10 NIV)

Toxic relationships hurt our spirits. Suffering people who lack hope also begin to despair. When suffering and in the dark about relief, people's rage turns to God. He is not harming us, but we are angry because we want Him to make it stop! We begin to lash out against God and reject His Word, which can help us. If we are not in fellowship with God, our trouble is the excuse for unbelief. If we are children of God, we may believe He has forsaken us. We forget that God has given humanity free will, and these clash with one another. Sin ruins people, and sin is why people ruin themselves and others.

God wants us to make blessed choices. Remember the psalmist lifting up his soul?

Read Psalm 25 again.

The psalmist was in trouble and trusted in God confidently to help him. We must learn to do this. I intentionally wrote this book for Christian people suffering in toxic relationships. If you are not a Christian and would like to be one who follows Christ, ask the Lord Jesus Christ to forgive you for your sin and save your soul. And if you do this, you are now a child of God!

> For God so loved the world that he gave his
> one and only begotten Son, that whoever believes
> in him shall not perish but have eternal life. (John
> 3:16 NIV)

God listens to and helps His children. This is not a promise of a trouble-free life!

Jesus overcame the world, and He shows us how to overcome also. Accepting God's salvation through Jesus Christ and learning life skills are blessed decisions we can make. God will support us. God will help us. God's love is the highest form of love we will ever experience. He will meet all our needs and fill those areas in our lives that we need help with. Through our spirits as children of God, we can ask for His help and know that He will help us!

The Serenity Prayer is powerful for helping people in difficult situations because it divides our work and God's work. This is so that we can do what we are responsible for and rest assured that God is also working. Millions of people have found strength in this short, twenty-five-word prayer.

The Serenity Prayer

God grant me the serenity to accept the things I cannot change, courage to change the things I can, and the wisdom to know the difference. (Reinhold Niebuhr)

Serenity is inner peace. This prayer begins with a request for inner peace and acceptance for the things we cannot change. We cannot change the moon, the stars, or the temperature of the sun. We do not argue or complain about why God made the sky blue and the grass green. We do not lose inner peace because gravity on Earth comes down. We are not angry because snow is white and blood is red. We cannot change our race. Oranges and apples are different, and so are every other species on this planet. Wishing, crying, fasting, praying, and hating God will not change an apple into an orange or even remove a zebra's stripes!

These things are as is in the universe, and there is nothing we can do about them. We accept these facts, get on with life, and concentrate on other things. We can peacefully accept that our NPS/toxic loved one is who they are and accept that we cannot to change them, nor should we try. We have to love them carefully and proactively. That is all that we can do, and know that it is not displeasing to God for us to protect ourselves from toxic people that we love. *Ask God to grant the serenity to accept that we cannot change the NPS/toxic person and let go of trying.*

A miracle will happen when we do this! Every miracle begins with our participation with God and releasing what we have to God.

Our lives will begin improving—exponentially! We will unleash our potential to change ourselves when we are finished trying to turn zebras into unicorns! Suddenly our hope is bright because we are not exhausted with what we cannot change. We become exhilarated with what we can change: ourselves! This is a refreshing state.

The next request in the Serenity Prayer is for courage to change what we can. I like to make lists. I find that if I organize my thoughts this way, I can shuffle my priorities around as needed. Try it. It may be helpful to you. List what you can change. Be honest. List the hard and easy things because you have freed up wasted energy that is now available to achieve your goals!

Courage is doing what must be done despite fear. We can only change ourselves, not others. We can improve our lives. It will take desire, courage, support, purpose, and the passion to continue on that path. God will help us with these things. We can choose not to worry about the miracles and work with what we have. We can accept that some things will stay as God made them, like the zebras. We can choose to heal by refusing to remain hurt. We can live with purpose instead of just existing. We can be the people God wants us to be. In healthy ways, we can find others that are good for us, and we can be that for them. We can choose to live better lives. We can choose to pray for, forgive, and let go of offenses. We can choose to experience peace.

The Serenity Prayer ends with a request to know the difference between the cannot-change and can-change items in life. Here is an example: If the toxic person you are breaking a relationship with is your sibling, you cannot change the fact that they are family. Because of their behavior, you have to love them carefully—that is, you have to create boundaries for interaction and communication. You may not be able to include them in your personal business that families usually share. You may have to not introduce them to other people in your life because of their antics. You are not hating them. You are loving them and not trying to change who they are. You are also protecting yourself.

You cannot change them. You have changed yourself by creating necessary boundaries. This takes courage, and you know the difference.

> You hear, O LORD, the desire of the afflicted;
> You encourage them, and you listen to their cry,
> defending the fatherless and the oppressed, in
> order that man, who is of the earth, may terrify
> no more. (Psalm 10:17–18 NIV)

CHAPTER 15

Up, Up, and Away!

I will exalt you, O LORD, for you lifted me
out of the depths and did not let my enemies
gloat over me. O LORD my God, I called to
you for help and you healed me. O LORD,
you brought me up from the grave; you
spared me from going down into the pit.
—Psalm 30:1–3 NIV

As we prepare for our exodus from NPS/toxic relationships, we must resolve to grow and improve ourselves while loving others enough to let them do the same and remembering valuable lessons.

We will enjoy freedom God's way—with power, love, and a sound mind. We will learn not to get entangled again. We will practice awareness, praying and paying attention. Should we still need help, we will confidently seek help from God (who is pleased to help us) and those who are relevant to our needs. We will remember that wherever there are gazelles, there are lions, and that's just part of life.

A critical change in transforming our lives is to stop conforming to the pattern of this world (Romans 12:2). We will stop practicing self-destructive mental habits and behaviors. The beginning of the end of this bond involves accepting the fact that we must stop using this toxic relationship because it is an addiction.

Most twelve-step recovery programs use the Serenity Prayer. The first thing on the list to help addicts have hope is seeking help from a *higher power*! Addiction is a loss of our personal power.

A power shift must take place! God's power must be infused into us and the situation to bring resolution and deliverance His way. With our focus on God, we will see light at the end of the tunnel. God will recharge us and fill us with new power to live free from this addiction.

The NPS/toxic person, like Pharaoh (in the story about Moses), can see and know the power of God but also may harden their hearts. Even believers who have narcissistic personality syndrome (NPS) understand wrong and right and know that there are consequences. They do not like rules or boundaries. They do not like consequences. They may even rebel against them as believers. The Lord knows how to deal with this behavior.

God does not tell us that we must be bound to believers with rebellion issues. Their souls may be saved because they accepted Christ, but Christ does not fight against their free will to rebel against Him. The long, painful reality is this: the NPS individual may struggle for the rest of their life because they must resolve to resist deeply embedded behavior patterns that are selfish, unempathetic, and harmful methods to please themselves. Yes, they are new creatures positionally, but they are who they are. Unless they completely yield to God, they will suffer their own harsh consequences regularly, and those close to them will suffer. They do not feel sympathy for those that they harm.

Antisocial behavior, doing wrong, and going into complete denial are reasons psychiatrists and God's hands are tied in helping the NPS individual.

Toxic-relationship martyrs are not virtuous for placing themselves in an NPS individual's path of destruction to "show God's love." God does not require us to self-destruct for other people's sins and disorders. Regardless of what condition anyone is in, we have to remember what God's Word says about sin and temptation and His intervention to help us with sin.

> No temptation has overtaken you except
> what is common to mankind. And God is faith-
> ful; He will not let you be tempted beyond what
> you can bear. But when you are tempted, He will
> also provide a way out so that you can endure it.
> (1 Corinthians 10:13 NIV)

Pray for them and live your life free from bondage. God will help them if they want it. God loves lifting people out of the pits of sin and bondage. He loves us more than we can ever understand. He is reaching out to all of us. If we take His hand, our lives will improve beyond our greatest dreams. God never said that blessings and freedom would be without a battle. Fighting our dysfunctions and learning better paths is a challenging, courageous learning course. It is not easy, but it's worth the struggle.

We must resist impatience with progress. If we trust in the Lord and do our part, we will discover that God has a divine timetable and knows how to piece our lives together into a beautiful fabric.

Everyone's toxic relationship is different. Each person will have to pray and allow the Lord to impress their own mind with the correct steps to safely remove themselves from the web. I said before that this book is largely for intimate relationships (i.e., romantic, marriage, dating), but it will help with all toxic relationships, including friends, coworkers, employers, family members, and relatives. Release everything to God and unburden your mind about whether anyone agrees with you or not.

Ask the Lord about what to do for your situation. One of the ways of God is that He offers relevant direction. He helped *Noah* build the ark and then told him how and when to get into it. The ark was fully prepared and stocked for the long voyage during and after the flood. God Himself shut the door to keep out those who did not contribute to the ark.

Joseph was directed by God through the jealous misdeeds of others—his brothers! He was sold into slavery, and God lifted him incrementally to affluence and power to fulfill his destiny as a ruler. His attitude was excellent. He saw his ordeal as a work of God to position him to save many lives during a seven-year famine.

Moses and Aaron were directed by God in how to end Israel's slavery in Egypt. Through a progression of awesome miracles ending with the Passover, Pharaoh and the Egyptians were happy to let Israel go! God opened up the Red Sea, making an impossible passage to freedom, and ruined those pursuing them. He will do the same for us.

CHAPTER 16

Recovery

*B*ECAUSE NPS AND *toxic relationships are an addiction, getting out and staying out is a struggle for many people. Repeating the same mistake becomes a painful life pattern if we do not change.* It does not matter how intelligent anyone is; a person may not recognize within themselves the addiction that causes repeat involvement and entanglement in NPS/toxic relationships.

I'll reinstate my belief that deep needs one does not know how to meet or will not meet for themselves causes this. Not knowing how to care for certain needs, especially love deficits, is frustrating. The solution seems so simple: find somebody to love (as the song says). But it is not that simple. Love is more than including someone in your life because of needs, sexual attraction, marriage, or what I call *palmenship.*

Palmenship is a dedicated commitment to a friendship that involves deeper love than friendly associations. David and Jonathan had a palmenship in the Bible. They were friends who were like close-knit brothers with a lifelong commitment to each other's good. Finding healthy people of this caliber is seriously getting more difficult these days. It is a sign of the times we are living in.

Recovery from addiction requires three stages of development, according to Fort Behavioral Health: *abstinence, repair, and growth* (fortbehavioral.com 2019). Toxic bonding is an addiction similar to drug addiction because it involves mental, emotional, and physical chemical dependence on DOSE. (Refer back to "Biological Bondage," chapter 9.) Recovery will be similar. Working through these stages is new behavior, so at first, it is natural to become impatient. We are in a hurry to feel better, but try to keep going through. Recovery takes time and is worth the effort. It paves the way to a beautiful new life. There is no quick fix.

Stage 1: abstinence

We have decided to stop a toxic relationship. We have asked God to help us. Now we must prepare to abstain from the toxic relationship. The closer the person is to you, the trickier it becomes to abstain from engaging them. People who do not live with you have the natural boundary of separate residences. Those you live with require a different approach.

Abstaining from toxic bonds does not imply rude behavior toward them or the silent treatment. It is a loving detachment. It is removing your intimate expectation and emotional connection from them. You will not expect them to meet your personal needs in life to the point of dependence and delusion to receive some benefits. You are taking responsibility for yourself and taking back personal power. It hurts because the old mental habit called this addiction and dependence love.

We must prepare to cope with what we wouldn't deal with before: self-care. The NPS individual will try and provoke you with jealousy to draw you back in, but continue taking care of yourself. A common thread in people chronically drawn to toxic others is a lack of self-care. This is deeper than dressing up or fitness. It is a personal-value issue. When we cut the toxic bond out of our life, sometimes the person is still around for some reason or another, and we need to stay free and well. Healing takes time in recovery, and sometimes healing is painful. I call this the pain of healing.

Stage 2: repair

The pain of healing involves correction and the time it takes to recover from that correction. I had major surgery once. A few weeks later, my incision began to smell weird, and it frightened me. My incision smelled like rotten fruit. I called the surgeon to have this checked. He laughed and said that the sweet-rotten smell was good. *It was a sign of deeper healing.*

Drainage and clean bandages would protect the area as healing continued. He also said that if it had smelled like roadkill, that would have been concerning because that was a symptom of a serious infection.

When we are recovering and healing, things may stink! During recovery, breaking old dysfunctional coping and mental habits is uncomfortable. Old issues that contribute to our dysfunctions usually have a painful origin connected to them. We must make peace with these.

Stage 3: growth

Developing excellent, new thought habits is important because withdrawal from toxic bonds tempts people to take the easy way out. Do not entangle yourself again! Guard your heart!

Here's an example: During abstaining from a toxic friendship, loneliness may try and tug you back in. You may reason, "This is my only friend." The lazy method to handle this is delusion. You think, *They are really fun to be with when they are not causing enormous amounts of trouble in my life.*

This is where asking some serious questions can help shift our behavior. "Why is this my only friend? Why didn't I try to make other healthier friends? How can I make healthier friends? Am I expecting friendship to give me personal value? Am I avoiding time with myself, and why?"

Now answer your questions with solutions. "I was afraid to make friends and settled for the first option that came along. I can pick and choose who to allow in my life. I will learn how to enjoy my own company, laugh at my mistakes, correct them, learn some social skills, and start enjoying life. I will not be afraid of not being somebody else's version of perfect. I can build healthy relationships."

Another way to prepare for abstaining from toxic bonds is joining a support group. Pray for and seek out a good support group. This may even be covered by your medical insurance. If you need treatment for conditions resulting from chronic stress, get it. This is medical care that is covered by HIPAA laws and protects your privacy.

Even though you may meet new people and see new things, resist the urge to form a rebound relationship. Recovery is not complete, and you do not need compound toxic bonding. We reap what we sow, and up to this point, we have been sowing toxic bonds. Sow recovery and new life skills that produce a desirable harvest in the future.

Understanding why we experience what we experience in our lives and adjusting ourselves to do better are a deposit on excellent living and loving.

When getting ready for recovery and during recovery, do not involve your audience. They are charmed by your NPS individual. The whole process must take place outside of those circles. This will also speed up healing because it cuts out the drama of close loved ones and friends who do not understand. The NPS individual invests in these people to keep you under control. Behind your back, they are doing many things to ensure the loyalty of this fan group. When you begin recovery, this is the first place they will seek to manipulate information and gain control from. New friends and acquaintances in your support groups will help fill this void. Keep them separate from your normal connections. God is also present to help and comfort you.

Keep enriching reading and audio materials available. Fill up your mind with good things and remind yourself that your life is improving because you are improving.

Physical withdrawal symptoms may come. If you are experiencing adrenal fatigue, little things may begin a panic attack. This is your body needing to readjust to normal levels of creating and dispensing adrenaline for emergencies. Breathe into a paper bag or your hands.

Deep breaths—about ten or fifteen—will stop this.

Next, get up and move around to get the extra adrenaline out of your body. Walk in place, do jumping jacks, go up and down the stairs, dance, rake leaves, sweep… Just move! As you get regular rest and exercise, your body will begin to regulate itself and release remaining excess built-up adrenaline from your body. Ask your doctor about taking magnesium. This inexpensive supplement calms the body and helps promote relaxation without drowsiness.

Dopamine, oxytocin, serotonin, and endorphin (DOSE) addiction needs replacement behaviors. Learn something new, begin a creative hobby, or visit beautiful places. Take a nice bubble bath or shower with a really nice body wash. Pray in beautiful places, walk, exercise, and volunteer. Go to a good church and participate. (Keep your situation between you and God; you do not want to have a toxic bond with a good organization.) These are small examples of pleasure-producing activities that you can look forward to that are nontoxic and fulfilling. Love-flood your own life. Pour into yourself what Scripture calls the healing balm—that which produces healing and protection. Allow God's love to flow through you, knowing that you are truly loved. Hug yourself.

CHAPTER 17

Cooperating with Recuperation

*He heals the brokenhearted and
binds up their wounds.*
—Psalm 147:3 NIV

*Recuperation is a period involving rest,
repairs and renewing ourselves.*

EXCELLENT RECOVERY—THAT IS, getting back to our best state—involves recuperation. In chapter 16, we began recovery and explored the pain of healing, the pain that occurs after removal or corrective actions. Psalm 147 has a two-part recuperation process for the brokenhearted.

First, God heals the brokenhearted

A sound mind is part of the healing of the heart. We know that some losses cannot be restored, such as lost time. And we cannot unkiss or unexperience what distressed us into heartbreak. All of that spilled milk is gone. We must give it all to God—completely!

We are going to feel sore for a while as our hearts heal. Surgery always involves going in deep to repair, and that involves pain. God is an excellent surgeon. He will help us become sound again. Soundness is wellness, strength, ability, and proper form. The pain subsides as we cooperate with our care plan. And it takes time for us to build new strength.

After surgery a nurse comes in to *check your vital signs.* Signs that indicate life are called vital signs. Heartbeat, pulse, temperature, and blood-pressure checks ensure things are getting back to normal. If anything is abnormal, it is given immediate attention, and they find out why it's abnormal. This is part of recuperation—monitoring for healthy vital signs. Are we living or just existing?

Pain management is part of healing. Responsible pain management involves understanding not only the source of the pain but also the qualities of what we use to manage that pain.

Doctors do not want their patients addicted to painkillers. Rebound relationships are like opioid pain relievers. They are addictive, dysfunctional-coping, and reentangling behaviors, the old patterns that required correction in the first place.

Rest and let healing take place. Continue whatever support you have in place. Make prayer, reflection on positive information, and the practice of new life skills your priorities. God will help us mitigate all losses. In the grief chapter, we will learn about the massive action (one decision) that speeds up deep healing.

Healing may involve scars. Scars are where damage was but is not anymore. Scars are the receipts of the healing process; otherwise, there would be festering wounds.

Second, God binds up our wounds

Properly closing up wounds after surgery is crucial for complete recovery. Medical procedures to close wounds depend on the nature of the wounds. Surgeons may suture (sew up), use medical glue, or employ a technique called cauterization (burning a wound close). Cauterization is interesting because it also removes undesirable growths (such as some cysts, warts, and certain tumors) besides desensitizing the wounded area.

God may have to remove something from our hearts or desensitize it to certain things to not only heal it but also make it better. Desensitizing does not mean blocking experiencing love but becoming unresponsive to NPS/toxic manipulation. God knows how to bind up (close up) our wounds.

Very soon after surgery, as we rest, recuperate, and manage pain, a medical worker and a therapist will come in to help get you up and moving.

Movement is just as important to recovery and recuperation as rest! Moving gets the blood flowing through our body, especially the wounded area, and produces muscle strength and repair; otherwise, we can form blood clots. Blood clots are dangerous and can be life-threatening! Blood clots in our situation are congealed, hardened unresolved areas that we need to work through and let go of. Forgiveness is the ultimate blood-clot resolver.

Lying down and not moving because we are hurting is only good when alternated with productive activity. The nurse will help you get up and move around daily. They might put compression garments and drains on you to help all the stuff that needs removal come out properly and hold in place what was operated on. Moving helps it all heal better.

Drains are the channels we release our toxic experience through. These built-up toxins must come out, and they decrease over time as healing takes place. This is why doctors measure drainage. If the body never reduces its drainage, that is a sign that deep healing is not happening. That's because with healing, drainage stops. I said this because never-ending complaining and constant murmuring and grumbling about our toxic experience are signs that deep healing is not happening.

I suggest that excessive grumbling about the situation should be avoided. Ignore it when it pops up in your thinking. Speak to yourself out loud and say, "God has healed me from that. I release hurtful memories to Him. I will not waste any more life engaging in it."

Then throw up a prayer, perhaps something like "Lord, thank You for healing my broken heart and binding up my wounds. Amen."

Cooperate with your recuperation plan because people who do not recover properly usually become ill again or worse! Keep your wounds clean as they heal.

Therapy is physical and mental. Moving those muscles and thoughts regularly and correctly builds strength, and before you know it, you will look and feel much better. Resist overdoing therapy because everything has to move through a process. Patiently work on and wait for your health and situation to improve. They are improving because you are improving with God's help.

> He gives strength to the weary and increases the power of the weak. Even youths grow tired and weary, and young men stumble and fall; but those who hope in the Lord will renew their strength. They will soar on wings like eagles; they will run and not grow weary, they will walk and not faint. (Isaiah 41:29–30 NIV)

CHAPTER 18

The Power of Forgiveness

Forgiveness is one of the most empowering decisions God has given man besides love and salvation. We must choose to love God, ourselves, and others. We must choose eternal life to accept God's love and salvation through Jesus Christ. We must choose to forgive and be forgiven. God gives us these choices. He does not interfere with our decisions.

God, in love, tells us the best way. He may even demonstrate why it's excellent. He will not force us to love, receive love, accept salvation, forgive, or be forgiven. God knows the effect of these excellent choices on the quality of our lives, but He does not force them.

> For He has rescued us from the domination
> of darkness and brought us into the kingdom of
> the Son He loves, in whom we have redemption,
> the forgiveness of sins. (Colossians 1:13–14 NIV)

Nothing seems to ruin life more than grief and heartbreak. When we are wronged, our lives seem to be dominated by the darkness of others' sinful offenses. This darkness is compounded by our wrong responses to our hurts and losses. We want the pain and suffering to stop. We want the person/s responsible for the hardship to understand the hurt and damages they caused in us and make things right. If they do not, will not, or cannot, we want them to pay a penalty. Even if they are penalized in some way, bitterness keeps fanning the flames until we catch fire and burn up in anger because of holding a grudge.

Vengeance and bitterness begin to affect our thinking and behavior. It affects our relationships with others. Bitterness changes how we interact with life; everything looks bleak. Gloom and anger smother out everything good that comes along. Our greatest achievements and prosperity turn to gravel in our mouths because we are mad at what happened to us. If our offender does well and doesn't seem to care that they hurt us, we dry up with resentment at their seemingly good fortune. It looks like they got away with wrong, and now we're tempted to do wrong!

Another waste of time is trying to show *them!* Nothing anyone does to impress offenders works because some have sunken so low to hurt us that we would have to go ten times lower for revenge. Now we will deserve ten times what we wish would happen to them for doing the same thing to us. Provoking jealousy in our offenders can backfire because often, they do not care.

Bitterness affects our relationship with God. If we are mad at God, things get even worse because we rage at the one who is able to help us the most. He loves us the most, but resentment blocks us from receiving God's love. God never does wrong, but He may have disappointed us because we wanted Him to do something and He didn't. God outperforms our greatest requests, but we may not see His blessings right away. So we hold unforgiveness toward God. We need to let go of all resentment and anger toward God.

We must also accept that we do not know all the mysterious ways that God works. He is not harming us, and we will never understand all the whys in life. We can ask God to help us with misunderstanding and anger toward Him, and He will help restore peace and faith in our hearts. God is blessing us, and He is always loving us.

Unforgiveness begins a course of acting out in anger and resentment as a lifestyle. Bitter people will begin punishing innocent people for what is not their fault, and that's because they are the only ones near. It is easy to project our offender's behavior onto people that mean no harm to us because we cannot get back at our true offender. It creates a dark paradigm that pollutes the future and, if unresolved, begins a chronic downward spiral of tremendous destruction and discontent.

Unforgiveness and bitterness also have another interesting consequence. They attract us to the same kind of person/s that hurt us before. This is because our mind is not only tightly focused on the offender, but also, the subconscious mind wants to overcome this situation like an antibody to a disease to prevent reinfection.

The stress of deep offense affects our bodies like a disease or serious infection. So the brain goes after the situation as such until it overcomes the threat! This is why unforgiveness turns destructive. It draws us back into the painful loop until we overcome it.

This is the poison that ruins us and others until there is nothing left but damages, damages, *damages*!

Unforgiveness is weak. It does nothing to help us. God gives us the most excellent way to healing and hope: forgive!

> Then said Jesus, Father, forgive them; for they know not what they do. And they parted his raiment, and cast lots. (Luke 23:34 KJV)

Imagine forgiving those who falsely accuse and condemn you. Christ's offenders were forgiven, but that didn't mean they were without consequences.

Adam and Eve were forgiven but not allowed back into the Garden of Eden.

Forgiveness releases our hearts so that we can do the next thing right, even dealing with our offenders. When we resolve not to carry the ball and chain of anger, resentment, and oppressive, hurtful memories; we clean our minds of festering damages that offense brings. Jesus is not teaching that we should be doormats for our enemies. He is teaching us how to practice an immediate response of not being dominated and controlled by pain and darkness. Seventy times seven is the perfect resolution to forgive. Release offense. Let it go!

> I cry to you, O LORD; I say, "You are my refuge, my portion in the land of the living. Listen

to my cry, for I am in desperate need; rescue
me from those who pursue me, for they are too
strong for me. Set me free from my prison, that
I may praise your name." (Psalm 142:5–6 NIV)

Depression and anger from deep hurt and offense feels like a prison. We feel locked in.

NPS targets are usually left high and dry without closure, apologies, answers or any warning.

The answers to riddling NPS behaviors are not forthcoming. Searching for answers consumes some targets hoping to make sense of what they have gone through and trying to figure out what to even call it.

The best thing is to forgive the wrong! Forgive what is and isn't known. God sees all and knows all. Trust in the Righteous Judge and let Him handle things. Trust God's righteousness with the mysteries; our mysteries are known to Him!

Forgiveness does not mean that if legal action is necessary, you do nothing. I knew a person once who was charmed by a toxic person. They ignored their gut each time God warned them. They thought the devil was accusing this really nice person. The person did so many great things in the community and for this family. Everyone thought highly of this individual. This person raped their twelve-year-old son, and when the family wanted to press charges, the organization he worked in said they should forgive the man and not press charges. The community couldn't handle the scandal. They discreetly pressed charges anyway and sought counseling for their son and family.

God never said forgiveness means that we acquit criminals, predators, or other dangerous people!

Keep me, O Lord, from the hands of the
wicked; protect me from men of violence. (Psalm
140:4 NIV)

The psalmist above prayed for God to keep him from the wicked. We can pray the same thing. We can pray for God to help us forgive and proceed under His direction. We can fix what we can, move forward in life with healed hearts and minds, and entrust ourselves to God.

Forgiveness positions us to receive forgiveness from God because we also sin. Unforgiveness makes us toxic because of the sin that results from a root of bitterness. We may not be murdering, raping, and stealing from others, but we fall short of God's will for us behaviorally at times. Sometimes we do the wrong thing—period! No excuse! Then we need forgiveness.

> Therefore confess your sins to each other and pray for each other so that you may be healed. The prayer of a righteous person is powerful and effective. (James 5:16 NIV)

Once trust is established with your counselor or support group, discussing issues and praying for one another is very healing. Do not disclose private information with your NPS/toxic person because they cannot be trusted, and you are trying to disconnect from them. Forgiving them does not mean that you are reengaged in the web their behavior has set for you. You do not hate, resent, begrudge, or take revenge on them. You accept that they are what and who they are but now cannot be in a relationship as you were before. You respond with wisdom and mitigate what you can. You also protect yourself in the future.

Forgiveness does not require us to renew broken trust in untrustworthy people or give undeserved trust to people at all. It does not require you to prove your forgiveness by opening yourself up to them again or reconciling. Forgiveness is releasing resentment and vengeance. This is being angry without sinning (Ephesians 4:26).

Jesus taught us to forgive when the person asks for forgiveness and offers repentance (i.e., stopping the wrong behavior).

> Even if that person wrongs you seven times a day and each time turns again and asks forgive-

ness, saying 'I repent," you must forgive him. (Luke 17:4 NLT)

Our NPS/toxic offenders may never apologize, feel remorse for their actions, or ask for forgiveness, but it is good to forgive anyway to unburden our minds. We make better decisions about our situations with clear thinking.

David ran from Saul for years, often after Saul apologized with tears in his eyes. David knew that a person could be sorry but not change their behavior because of deeper issues that cause the behavior.

Proactive, careful love and forgiveness saved David's life. David stayed away from Saul, and Saul repeatedly went into a rage and resumed his pursuit to kill David.

David forgave King Saul and protected himself.

When people teach forgiveness, they frequently skip over the part about the offender asking for forgiveness and repentance. Jesus never commanded us to just pass out forgiveness or ignore people's issues causing the problem behaviors.

> Now while he was in Jerusalem at the Passover Feast, many people saw the miraculous signs he was doing and believed in his name. But Jesus would not entrust himself to them, for he knew all men. He did not need man's testimony about man, for he knew what was in man. (John 2:23–25 NIV)

Jesus continued His work without putting Himself into the hands of people. He knew they were sinners and untrustworthy. He loved everyone carefully without being sidetracked by their sin. Jesus made a decision to protect Himself many times until it was time to go to the cross because He came to earth to die for our sins and then rise again for our victory and ensure eternal life. Until that time, Jesus protected Himself from harm.

The devastation of NPS relationships looks like New Orleans after Hurricane Katrina—massive devastation everywhere! The ruins are overwhelming to us, but they are not overwhelming to God. Remember, to heal we must deal with the rubble. It must be removed, recycled, or repurposed. Unforgiveness just holds on to the damages. Forgiveness sees the mess and losses and seeks ways to make things better. Unforgiveness locks us into the damages. Forgiveness releases the possibilities, blessings, and power to build a better future.

CHAPTER 19

Moving through Grief

*The Israelites grieved for Moses in the
plains of Moab thirty days, until the time
of weeping and mourning was over.*
—Deuteronomy 34:8

*After the death of Moses the servant of the LORD,
the LORD said to Joshua son of Nun, Moses'
aide: "Moses, my servant is dead. Now then,
you and all these people, get ready to cross the
Jordan River into the land I am about to give to
them to the Israelites.... Have I not commanded
you? Be strong and courageous. Do not be
terrified; do not be discouraged, for the LORD
your God will be with you wherever you go."*
—Joshua 1:1–2, 1:9 NIV

I HAVE SEEN PEOPLE go through NPS relationships and stay stuck in grief and shock for many years. Some believe that God will snap them out of grief. God understands the nature of grief; Jesus wept! He helps us move on. God walks with us through this valley—*through*!

> Yea, though I walk through the valley of the
> shadow of death, I will fear no evil: for thou art
> with me; thy rod and thy staff they comfort me.
> (Psalm 23:4 KJV)

We must move through grief with patience, wisdom, and hope. I am not going to expound on the stages of grief. It is like water. It has waves and tides, and it moves. Water that does not keep moving is foul because it needs movement to remain fresh and support life. Keep moving through with God.

The time of mourning is a heavy, temporary period. We must leave and move forward no matter how we feel toward God's promised land.

I like this passage because of how God walked Israel through grief. I am not a theologian, but I read this story and interpret it like this. *It appears that Israel has a set period specifically for weeping and mourning: thirty days.* It didn't say or imply that all emotional pain ceased after thirty days. Thirty days was a period to sit still and mourn. It is like putting a cast on a broken limb. Sit still and let your broken heart heal a while. Let it be immobile but not for too long. The cast must come off to prepare for movement again.

Expressing sadness, remorse, and other feelings following the death or loss of someone/something is mourning. Funerals and memorials are part of closure for death. Some cultures even employ wailing women to cry and weep loudly so that others can do the same and release the physical response to their loss. It can be comforting to have a closure ceremony with or without others to mourn a loss or failed relationship.

The relationship that we idealized is dead. If we pronounce it dead, we can plan to lay it to rest. Medical authorities usually pronounce deaths. First, they note the time that the person is unresponsive and under what circumstances. Then they check their vital signs: respiration, heartbeat, optical reflex, and pulse. If these are absent, they may test again. Finally, they note the final results of the tests and pronounce that time as the time of death if vital signs are absent. A death report and autopsy request are in order. The person is officially dead.

In dead relationships, we can usually estimate the time it became sick to the point of death, and once dead it is hopeless. We mourn. We desire closure and comfort. We want to be surrounded by support and loved ones. This is difficult for NPS targets; their closest loved ones are the audience and charmed by the NPS individual. So closure can be a lonely but necessary experience.

Dead toxic relationships are the ones when a target stops idealizing and hoping their fantasy is true, and they take a nice, hard look at the fruit on the tree and call it whatever it is! Jesus said we can look at the fruit a tree produces and know if that tree is good or bad. Good trees will not produce bad fruit. Bad trees will not produce good fruit. No fruit on a fruit tree is also a sign that it is useless and needs removing.

When mourning a dead relationship, close it out with care. Plan at least a thirty-day period to mourn your loss. Writing a private letter stating the cause of death and a few obituary-type words about the relationship can be helpful. If there are a few people that are outside the audience or part of your support group that you can do this with, it helps. Be as elaborate as you want. This is not done to the NPS individual or around them. We are not enemies, taking vengeance, publicly disgracing them, or fighting. We are detaching and moving on. We are mourning what was lost without sinful anger or disrespect. We are detaching ourselves with love and assertion. Saying a prayer, singing a song, or reading a poem or a scripture is helpful during your closure service.

My favorite detachment document is the Declaration of Independence. This powerful, eloquent, and explicit document is the best breakup letter ever written! The points and explanations as to why the detachment is happening are noted and signed by our country's founding fathers.

After thirty days of weeping and mourning, it is time to prepare to move forward. It is important to have a move-on date because it gives us a goal, a focus, and it motivates us to take positive action toward the future. Getting stuck in the barren land of grief is easy to do, especially if we believe we still have something important there to bring along.

This is when you look at your vital signs to see if there really is life! Unless God Himself tells you there is going to be a miraculous relationship resurrection, the relationship's death certificate is proof that it is time to move forward.

Move toward the future with courage and faith! God used Joshua to lead Israel to the Promised Land. This was their destination after leaving bondage in Egypt.

It takes courage to move forward! Refuse to be discouraged or terrified. God commands this. It is easier to obey God's command than to try and convince oneself. Obey God and move forward. On the journey through grief, we will find that it is a period of personal discovery, growth, cleansing, reflection, and healing. Carry on.

As we are moving toward the future, we are pushing through the rubble of our ruins. Remember the rubble in chapter 18, on forgiveness? After the catastrophe are ruins. Understanding what we value helps during mourning. We must ask ourselves questions: "What have I lost? How was it lost? Why was it so valuable? What can I do about it? When can I do something about it? Where can I go for support? Where do I go from here?"

There is a difference between mourning and grief. We just talked about mourning, which is expressing grief outwardly. Knowing the difference between mourning and grief can help us understand where we stand in the process. No one experiences grief or mourning without a loss. The loss was valuable to us; otherwise, it wouldn't have saddened us. Alan Wolfelt of the TAPS organization stated, "Think of grief as a container. It holds your thoughts and feelings and images of your experience when someone you love dies. In other words, grief is the internal meaning given to the experience of loss" (Wolfelt 2018, taps.org).

What did this loss mean to you personally? Grieving with wisdom is important if we want to get through it. Idealized relationships for targets usually are some expectation for fulfillment that we hoped another would contribute to support our needs. These needs are those we need to learn to meet for ourselves. Songs like "You're Nobody 'til

Somebody Loves You" feed the dissatisfaction of singleness because it implies worthlessness. Truthfully, we are not ready to share our lives until we as individuals can live a balanced, content life.

We should not grieve selfishly. Our losses also affect others who really care for and support us. They idealized the relationship with us because they hoped for our best. They wanted us to be happy. We must remember that they are hurting also when we hurt. People who pour time and effort into helping us deserve closure also. Some bonding happened between them and the toxic person by proximity. Consider this for those who may have to completely sever their relationship with this person. Other relationships where we are detached but still communicating with caution can be less severe and have less grief.

People directly affected by our dysfunctional relationships and have the least say are usually children. It is extremely important to consider children's feelings when we grieve. They may have loved the person we need to detach from, and it is harder to explain things explicitly to them. If it is a parent, sibling, close friend, or other near relative, age-appropriate explanations are necessary. Do not try to infuse hate into the children to punish the offender.

These must be thought out carefully. We are not trying to add the burden of hate onto children. Hate breeds more hate and will backfire.

Here's an example: We can say, "So-and-so has a problem with getting into trouble with the police. They are not allowed to hang out with us because they are always doing illegal things. We do not hate them, but we do not want to get blamed for what they do and go to jail. We will pray for them to make better choices." Figure out your explanation on paper, then share it. Most kids can grasp this. Never lie on or bad-mouth the person you are detaching from.

Grieving is a time for cleansing. When we search for our whys, we dig through the ruins, looking for answers. And we find some answers. We begin to discover things we forgot about that were neglected or overindulged. We pull out all the junk from the piles and are amazed at the hoard of things, mostly unnecessary things, filling up our lives. Where did all this stuff come from? Bad behaviors, bad choices, wasteful habits, laziness, workaholism, erroneous ideas about life, powerlessness, or faux omnipotence, fantasy, and truth. Whenever you see a cleanup site after ruins, the construction workers separate everything into relevant piles to decide what can be reused to help rebuild. The other things may be trash, sold, or headed for the landfill. Once everything is separated and the junk is hauled off, it is amazing how beautiful everything is. When our lives are cleared of debris, it becomes a clean canvas to begin anew.

With the lessons we learned, we can build better. After cleaning up the ruins, keep clean! As we grieve, we realize that we have lost energy, life, money, good relationships, and valuable time. We are sad. We learn to reach out to God to help us and patiently help ourselves. We reflect on what we thought we had, and we let others do the same. Forgiveness helps us reflect without bitterness.

If we must let go of some tangible things, we will do so with a positive attitude, not anger or bitterness. Holding on to tangibles is a form of attachment, so let go of stuff that keeps you connected where you need to detach. With a heart full of forgiveness, let go of the remains. Do not let people reinfect you with hurt, anger, and unforgiveness. Let it all go! Life will brighten up soon! Visualize yourself happy again, because you will be. God will fill your life with good things.

> The Spirit of the Sovereign LORD is on me, because the LORD has anointed me to preach good news to the poor. He has sent me to bind up the brokenhearted, to proclaim freedom for the captives and release from darkness for the prisoners, to proclaim the year of the LORD's favor and the day of vengeance of our God, to comfort all who mourn, and provide for those in Zion to bestow on them a crown of beauty instead of ashes, the oil of gladness instead of mourning, and a garment of praise instead of a spirit of despair. They will be called oaks of righteousness, a planting of the LORD for the display of His splendor. They will rebuild the ancient

ruins and restore the places long devastated; they will renew the ruined cities that have been devastated for generations. Instead of their shame my people will receive a double portion, and instead of disgrace they will rejoice in their inheritance; and so they will inherit a double portion in their land, and everlasting joy will be theirs. (Isaiah 61:1–4, 61:7 NIV)

It takes diligent work to rebuild ruined cities. Enjoy the journey instead of dreading the task.

Anxiety and impatience will tempt you to take shortcuts, and the shortcut always cuts you short! Do not sell out your opportunity to build and have a better life because you want instant gratification. Let patience finish what she is doing so that you will be completely whole and lacking nothing. Ask God for wisdom and trust Him to give you all the wisdom that you need. Do not be double-minded or two-faced with God, because you will be unstable and receive nothing, and it will be your own fault. *This is my version of James 1:4–8.*

CHAPTER 20

Reconstruction

*"For I know the plans I have for you," declares
the LORD, "plans to prosper you and not harm
you, plans to give you hope and a future."*
—Jeremiah 29:11 NIV

THIS WAS PART of the message the Lord sent to His people in exile from Jerusalem in Babylon by the prophet Jeremiah. The people were anxious to get on with life after being freed from Babylonian rule. God wanted them to stay still and use the resources already at their disposal. Everyone cannot jump up and immediately relocate to live their best life wherever they want. But we can begin living our best lives wherever we are!

Do what you can where you are with what
you have. (Theodore Roosevelt)

Moving on and rebuilding our lives is something everyone will do differently because we are all different and in different situations. We can rebuild with whatever we have right now! Moving in the right direction, forward, is very motivating, and our brains need the joy of achievement. According to the late radio host Earl Nightingale, success is taking the first step toward our goals.

In the previous chapter, we see God telling Israel at the end of thirty days, the period for weeping and mourning, to get ready to move on. It is wise to consider preparations to live better. It is time to transition from grieving and mourning to obtaining God's blessings for us in our promised land.

The promised land may be right where you are! God may want you to prosper in the area you suffered in. He might change things in your favor. The Lord moved things around in Babylonia to free His people in exile there. Pray for direction and help to do what is best for you in your situation before making drastic changes. God has a plan for His people wherever we are, even in places we do not want to be. Check with the Lord and do what He says.

> This is what the LORD Almighty, the God of Israel, says to all those I carried into exile from Jerusalem to Babylon: "Build houses and settle down; plant gardens and eat what they produce. Marry and have sons and daughters; find wives for your sons and give your daughters in marriage, so that they too may have sons and daughters. Increase in number there; do not decrease. Also, seek the peace and prosperity of the city to which I have carried you into exile. Pray to the LORD for it, because if it prospers, you too will prosper." (Jeremiah 29:4–7 NIV)

Wow! What an encouraging command. God wants them to stay where they are, even as exiles, and prosper! He is giving the order to do this. It doesn't matter that some want to go out because they are anxious. Even after Israel was delivered from Pharaoh and slavery in Egypt, God took them through an impossible way to prevent war. He did not want the transition from being slaves to free men to be overwhelming. God sent them the long way, and the Red Sea was the only obstacle. God opened up the obstacle and created a miraculous passage.

As you rebuild your life after your hardship, God will strengthen and direct you along the best paths to grow and care for yourself. This is not the time to try and impress others or jump into another intimate relationship right away.

Now we proceed with caution. Make sure we are not toxically bonding. Finding our resources or enriching those resources that we already have will be a catalyst for our new life. If the Lord tells you to remain where you are, He will give you wisdom about how to live there. Joseph didn't ask to be sold into slavery by his brothers. In the land of his suffering, God raised him up to be the second ruler in all the land, next to Pharaoh. This was his destiny.

> The LORD will guide you always; He will satisfy your needs in a sun-scorched land and will strengthen your frame. You will be like a well-watered garden, like a spring whose waters never fail. (Isaiah 58:11 NIV)

Cambridge Dictionary defines *reconstruction* as the process of building or creating something again that has been damaged or destroyed (dictionary.cambridge.org). *God is the Master Rebuilder!* Ruined lives are His specialty! He is able to supply impossible needs, even the needs of the NPS individual! In God they have the never-ending supply of everything they need. We cannot make them receive this, and God does not force Himself either. The Lord is available to help everyone in need.

If the Lord leads you to separate from your NPS loved one, do it trusting in the Lord for whatever you thought that person could provide. God can and will do greater.

Abram was sent away from his home of origin. God commanded him to leave his father's house and relatives and to go to a land He would show him. Abram started walking into the unknown, and God took care of him and blessed him the entire way. Abram was renamed Abraham, and he made mistakes. But God continued helping him. Part of Abraham's blessing was that as he walked and trusted in God, he was blessed with a new identity that reflected the purpose God had for him and his wife, Sarai. She was renamed Sarah.

This barren couple became parents beyond all hope at about a century old. They miraculously conceived and gave birth to Isaac. His is the line from which our Savior, Jesus Christ, would descend. God provided for them in lands they had never known and was promised land—a new territory from God.

God will lead us always, and we should obey Him always. He will satisfy our needs in a sun-scorched land. When things are drying up or have dried up, God will still miraculously provide for us. He is promising not just material needs but also all our needs as humans. People need a relationship with God and others, and people need a healthy self-perspective and purpose. We need love, joy, peace, activity, and rest. We need food, clothing, shelter, and meaningful work. God knows how to place us in wonderful places, and He helps us grow and be productive where He places us. We can build our homes on *the rock*!

> Forget the former things; do not dwell on the past. See I am doing a new thing! Now it springs up; do you not perceive it? I am making a way in the desert and streams in the wasteland. (Isaiah 43:18–19 NIV)

AFTERWORD

I HOPE THIS BOOK *is a tremendous blessing to you.* May the Lord bless, keep, and protect you. May He direct you through this difficult time in your life. May He lift you up and out of the web of deception, exploitation, hurt, and danger. May He help your loved ones (including the NPS/toxic individual) know Him in a rich and saving way. May He help you love and value yourself correctly. May the Lord lift your continence to that of the joyful and fill you to overflowing with His love, peace, healing, prosperity, His presence, and more power!

If you do not know the Lord, please receive His salvation through Jesus Christ and the forgiveness of your sins. God loves you and has great plans for you. He will supply all your needs.

God bless you,
Marcella Detreville

ABOUT THE AUTHOR

Marcella Detreville writes from her personal experiences and biblical and secular research to encourage and comfort others with the insight and comfort God has given her through her life's difficulties.

She does a compelling job of explaining the dynamics of intimate narcissistic-personality-syndrome (NPS) relationships and how to recover from them.

Her book helps individuals analyze themselves to have a powerful effect on their own circumstances and, more importantly, their future. Freedom, happiness, and hope are available for those who read this book and apply the information to their situation.

She believes that changed thinking changes things.

Marcella's favorite Scripture is Romans 12:2, specifically in the Today's English Version: "Do not conform yourselves to the standards of this world, but let God transform you inwardly by a complete change of your mind. Then you will be able to know the will of God—what is good and pleasing to Him and is perfect."